AF454180

This Man Was Right

Woodrow Wilson Speaks Again

Hugh J. Schonfield

Across the span of two world wars comes a voice that the peacemakers, this time must heed

THIS MAN WAS RIGHT

Woodrow Wilson Speaks Again

DEDICATED TO

THE SERVICE—NATION MOVEMENT WITH ITS
WILSONIAN IDEALS OF SERVICE, MEDIATION AND
EXAMPLE.

This edition edited by Stephen A. Engelking

ISBN: 978-3-949197-07-9

Originally published in 1943 as a booklet by W.H. Allen
& Coy., Ltd., London.

Photograph of Woodrow Wilson from the Harris &
Ewing Collection at the Library of Congress

THIS MAN WAS RIGHT

A Collection of Extracts from Addresses given from 1913-1918 by President James Woodrow Wilson appropriate to the Present Time

Arranged with an Introduction

by

HUGH J. SCHONFIELD

"By faith Abel offered unto God a more excellent sacrifice than Cain, by which he obtained witness that he was righteous, God testifying of his gifts; and by it HE BEING DEAD YET SPEAKETH. "

Hebrews xi. 4.

"Woodrow Wilson gave up his health and eventually his life in the first attempt, a generation ago, to preserve the world's peace through united world action. At that time, there were many who said that Wilson had failed. Now we know that it was the world that failed, and the suffering and war of the last few years is the penalty it is paying for its failure.... Now at last the nations of the world have a second chance to erect a lasting structure of peace —a structure such as that which Woodrow Wilson sought to build but which crumbled away because the world was not yet ready. Wilson himself foresaw that it was certain to be re-built some day. This is related by Josephus Daniels in his book. The Life of Woodrow Wilson, as follows:

> Wilson never knew defeat, for defeat never comes to any man until he admits it. Not long before the close of his life Woodrow Wilson said to a friend: 'Do not trouble about the things we have fought for. They are sure to prevail. They are only delayed.' With the quaintness which gave charm to his sayings he added: 'And I will make this concession to Providence—it may come in a better way than we propose. '"

HENRY A. WALLACE, *Vice-President of the United States.*

From an address given on December 28, 1942, the eighty-sixth anniversary of the birth of Woodrow Wilson, under the auspices of the Woodrow Wilson foundation.

Contents

Introduction

There are great and generally understood differences between World War No. 2 and World War No. 1; but there are far greater and more striking similarities. Because of this there has been a tendency in certain quarters to play down these likenesses in order to invest the present struggle with an atmosphere of novelty, both as to its character and aims, in the interest of a maximum war effort, and to minimise the depressing effect of a second world war in twenty-five years, when the first was to have achieved the end of all war and a permanent international order.

It is natural, especially for older people, to feel that the conflict which now rages is but episode two of one and the same war, with the same principal foe and an almost identical array of allies in the camp of the United Nations. And, after all, the chief difference lies in the fact that World War No. 1 was an unprecedented experience. Public opinion is not to be blamed if mindful of the failure of statesmen—with a clear field—to carry out the promises and realize the ideals of the former occasion it is somewhat sceptical as to the prospects of fulfilment of the only slightly varied purposes proclaimed by statesmen this time. Many people think that they will again be let down by their governments, and that World War No. 3 will be the inevitable sequel.

The statesmen ought to be more conscious than they appear to be of this prevalent feeling, and they in particular should heed the words of Woodrow Wilson, who, in this volume, speaks to them and to the world again. It is a matter of personal judgment whether any of the present leaders is his equal in mental stature and vision. Certainly none is his superior.

Of course it may be urged that having a second chance we shall do better because we shall profit by our past mistakes. Knowing in what we went wrong then, we shall be wiser in our planning, more determined and unselfish in our actions, more fully alive in every way to our opportunities and responsibilities. But there is little that has transpired so far to encourage an optimistic view. Rather does leadership, in the political domain, with a few notable exceptions, still seem to be in the hands of the old discredited firm of Blimp, Bourbon and Co., who have learned nothing and forgotten nothing.

However, there is *the chance*; and in the hope of in some small way improving it this record has been compiled. For nothing emerges more clearly from it than its topicality today. Let it be the care of those who are prone to stress the distinctions between our two world wars. To study its pages; they will be surprised at the frequency of themes and phrases which, on the lips of our present spokesmen, are supposedly new, and uttered with all the conviction of originality. How little in fact has changed, how much is but a feeble echo! Even the terms in which German delinquency are described might be reported from current speeches. It has been the function of the editor to heighten the effect of this insistent topicality in the Divisions and Sub-Headings, and the Index of Notable Passages, and of course in his actual selection of the extracts. But, indeed, all that has been included might have been spoken by a man still with us in the flesh directly to our own time and circumstances, and in answer to our own questions and longings. For Woodrow Wilson is entitled to be called a prophet, and it is in the nature of prophetic messages that they often fall more aptly upon the ears of later generations than upon those of contemporaries.

Wilson was before his time, and his time did not understand him as we can understand him, and learn of him. This too is in the prophetic tradition. And we are the more eager to learn and understand because the consequences of heedlessness to his warnings and lack of resolution to realize his visions are matters of history. In possession of the tragic knowledge, which already shadowed his last years on earth, and indeed killed him, we could weep poignant tears, less for him than for ourselves, tears such as angels weep. But are these tears of mortified pride only, or of sincere repentance and promise of amendment?

For millions nowadays, however, Woodrow Wilson is just the name of the Democratic President of the United

States during World War No. 1; he is not even a memory. His burning and eloquent words do not lose any of their force and appropriateness thereby, and they may have gained the quality of revelation as they are read for the first time. But a few basic facts about him will not detract from the impression created by his addresses.

James Woodrow Wilson was born in 1856, and in his earlier career, except for his legal capacity and interest in American history, he gave few indications of the great statesman he was to become in later life. From 1902-1910 he was President of Princeton University, and he was in the middle fifties when he took public office as Governor of New Jersey from 1910-1912. In the latter year he entered into a triangular fight for the U. S. Presidency, and succeeded in defeating both Taft and Theodore Roosevelt.

Previous to his election he had shown no special concern for international problems, though the idea of the Hague Courts had rather appealed to him. Now he was summoned almost abruptly to occupy the centre of a world stage which he had had no hand in setting, and to play a principal part which was alien to all his inclinations. Just before he went to the White House he had said: "It would be the irony of fate if my administration had to deal chiefly with foreign affairs." Yet this fate was what destiny had in store for him, and at the most fateful period of history.

When war broke out in Europe in 1914 the crisis electrified Wilson. He saw it from the very beginning as the crisis of modern civilisation. All the ideals which were the mainspring of American national life as exhibited in the Declaration of Independence and the Bill of Rights were in the melting pot. Unless they emerged untarnished, and indeed enhanced by becoming universal, there was an end of America and of the cause of Liberty everywhere. The United States, therefore, personified in himself, not only could not stand aside but had a manifest duty and responsibility to be the mouthpiece of all peoples struggling for freedom against oppression. Wilson became the incarnate spirit of righteousness and judgment, with an unerring penetration of the shams and special pleadings with which the belligerents in varying degree sought to disguise the motives which actuated them. He challenged imperialism in the name of all subject races. He denied that the old imperialistic policy, or balance of power alliances, had any validity for the world of to-day, that governments had the right to act without the unqualified assent of the people they governed; and he discerned clearly and stated plainly that war such as this was intolerable unless it destroyed war for ever. Wilson would have no lesser results than absolute and openhanded fair dealing for all men and all nations, deliverance from fear of aggression, economic and social justice, and a permanent peace secured through the reign of law. He became the champion of the Rights of Man.

The effect of Wilson's dynamic utterances has been ably summarised by W. E. Woodward: but because he was writing in the midst of our own pre-war crisis his conclusions betray some of that cynicism which in these years has infected so many. "Here," says this author of A New American History (pp 601 - 602), "we have a college professor who will capture and hold the attention of all mankind. The people of the world will listen to his words as though he were an oracle speaking eternal truths. Despised and half-forgotten races will be thrilled by his name. He will be hailed as the saviour of men. Then we shall see his triumphs turn to ashes, wet with hopeless tears... The overwhelming disaster of his life came from his conviction that men are reasonable beings, that right and justice, sustained of course by logic, must win in the end. Such noble conceptions are not supported by experience, unfortunately. If the human race were inspired by logic and a sense of justice the great social problems that confront civilization would be solved in a few years. He was half blinded by looking upward at the stars, and it was his misfortune that he attempted to translate celestial ideals into terrestrial phenomena."

Such comment is not quite fair; or, if it be thought fair, what becomes of President Roosevelt's Four Freedoms, the Atlantic Charter, and all the other declarations and programmes that renew our encouragement to strive upwards to the stars? Are there never to be days of heaven upon earth?

Wilson was re-elected for a second term in 1916, and resumed office just before the entry of the United States into the war. He was succeeded by Harding in 1920 after his failure to secure the full co-operation for his Peace Programme of the Allied statesmen, and to carry the vote of the Senate for the Peace Treaties and participation in the League of Nations. He died on February 3, 1924, a broken man physically and mentally.

But who shall say that Wilson's great mission was not accomplished? He had lit a torch than can never be extinguished while men believe in the abiding principles for which he stood. The evidence of his speeches shows no wilful blindness to the weaknesses of human nature, or lack of perception of the tortuous ways of politicians. He knew that he was issuing a challenge to do the big thing and the right thing to men whose training and background might prevent them from responding adequately. That is why he appealed directly to the people to goad their rulers along the straight and narrow path which they would not walk voluntarily. That is why in fundamental things he used exceeding plainness of speech, covering the same ground again and again. He was admittedly a logician. Studying his language we come upon one word, his favourite, constantly repeated: it is "process." He saw the affairs of men and nations as a process, working out through inexorable laws. The completion might be delayed; but it was none the less inevitable. He had the natural desire of all mortals to see a partial fulfilment, at least, in his own time. And in this, as in the experience of other great leaders and prophets, he was disappointed. The Promised Land was not for the treading of his wearied feet.

Nearly all that Wilson said still remains true. It has a more weighty and conscience-pricking import now than when he spoke. It seems, indeed, that it was for us and to us that he was speaking. It may seem even more so to a generation beyond ours if we arc apathetic and therefore fail. But we need not fail. That is why this Volume purposely ends on the eve of Wilson's setting out for Europe to attend the Peace Conferences. Like the Apostle Paul, he might have told his friends: "And now, behold, I go bound in the spirit unto Jerusalem, not knowing the things that shall befall me there." It deliberately allows a great question mark to hang over the sequel, a ghostly question mark, materialising again in these days with increasing definition with the passing of every fateful hour that brings us nearer to the corresponding moment, to our own handling of essentially the same problems.

It remains briefly to describe the structure of this book and the material employed in it. The grouping of the extracts into six divisions has been undertaken by the editor in order to bring together under appropriate and currently used titles the statements of Woodrow Wilson on various occasions and over a period of six years, from 1913 to 1918. The quotations in each division are in chronological sequence, and therefore preserve the progress of thought on each theme; but while this means a going backwards and forwards the order of the divisions has been arranged so as to provide as far as possible a coherent and developing thesis which reaches a climax with the final passages. It has not been easy to make these divisions, and a certain amount of overlapping has been unavoidable; but none of the extracts is distributed between two divisions, and as far as quotation goes each is complete in itself. The sub-headings again are those of the editor, designed as an aid to the selection of subjects and convenience of reading. The unusual course has been followed of putting an Index of Notable Passages at the beginning of the book, for reasons already stated, to heighten the topical impression.

Most of the material consists of Public Addresses, and the greater part were issued at the time in pamphlet form by the President's office. During the period also various collections were published in America, and that which the present editor has particularly made use of is Albert Bushnell Hart's edition of Selected Addresses and Public Papers of Woodrow Wilson compiled in 1918. A very few items are from Press reports, and the two communications through Secretary Lansing are known to have been in the main Wilson's composition. The editor owes to Mr. Hart the date and occasion of each extract printed at its close: but is not otherwise indebted to him as to form or content. This book, indeed, is designed to serve a very different purpose, and the selection of the material and the length of the extracts has been an un-aided choice. Instead of being for domestic consumption, covering a very wide range of themes, many of them of major interest to Americans, it is directed to meet the re-quirements of a world situation, truly of concern to Americans, but just as much to all the Democracies, a situation which not only had not then arisen—or rather was being concluded—but which it was fondly hoped would never arise again. It is that resurrection which makes this edition so vitally necessary. A limited number of the addresses has been given in full; but otherwise the extracts are sufficient to cover the passages pertinent to our purpose, and to place many remembered and famous sayings within the framework of their context.

Index of Notable Passages

Index of Notable Passages

"The tragical events of the thirty months of vital turmoil through which we have just passed have made us citizens of the world".....................112

"These great ends cannot be achieved by debating and seeking to reconcile and accommodate what statesmen may wish with their projects for balances of power and of national opportunity. They can be realized only by the determination of what the thinking peoples of the world desire, with their longing hope for justice and for social freedom and opportunity"..........................116

"Germany will have to redeem her character, not by what happens at the peace table but by what follows...".......119

"the air every now and again gets darkened by mists and groundless doubtings and mischievous perversions of counsel"....................122

"this is a peoples' war, not a statesman's. Statesmen must follow the clarified common thought or be broken"
....................123

"plain workaday people have demanded, almost every time they came together, and are still demanding, that the leaders of their Governments declare to them plainly

I. Freedom and Democracy

Sovereignty of the People

The people of a democracy are not related to their rulers as subjects are related to a government. They are themselves the sovereign authority, and as they are neighbours of each other, quickened by the same influences and moved by the some motives, they can understand each other. They are shot through with some of the deepest and profoundest instincts of human sympathy. They choose their governments; they select their rulers; they live their own life, and they will not have that life disturbed and discoloured by fraternal misunderstandings. I know that a reuniting of spirits like this can take place more quickly in our time than in any other because men are now united by an easier transmission of those influences which make up the foundations of peace and of mutual understanding, but no process can work these effects unless there is a conducting medium. The conducting medium in this instance is the united heart of a great people.

Address at a Monument in Memory of the Confederate Dead at Arlington, June 4, 1914.

Liberty versus Autocracy

A steadfast concert for peace can never be maintained except by a partnership of democratic nations. No autocratic government could be trusted to keep faith within it or observe its covenants. It must be a league of honour, a partnership of opinion. Intrigue would eat its vitals away; the plottings of inner circles who could plan what they would and render account to no one would be a corruption seated at its very heart. Only free peoples can hold their purpose and their honour steady to a common end and prefer the interests of mankind to any narrow interest of their own.

Does not every American feel that assurance has been added to our hope for the future peace of the world by the wonderful and heartening things that have been happening within the last few weeks in Russia? Russia was known by those who knew it best to have been always in fact democratic at heart, in all the vital habits of her thought, in all the intimate relationships of her people that spoke their natural instinct, their habitual attitude towards life. The autocracy that crowned the summit of her political structure, long as it had stood and terrible as was the reality of its power, was not in fact Russian in origin, character, or purpose; and now it has been shaken off and the great, generous Russian people have been added in all their naive majesty and might to the forces that are fighting for freedom in the world, for justice, and for peace. Here is a fit partner for a League of Honour.

One of the things that has served to convince us that the Prussian autocracy was not and could never be our friend is that from the very outset of the present war it has filled our unsuspecting communities and even our offices of government with spies and set criminal intrigues everywhere afoot against our national unity of counsel, our peace within and without, our industries and our commerce....

We are accepting this challenge of hostile purpose because we know that in such a government, following such methods, we can never have a friend; and that in the presence of its organized power, always lying in wait to accomplish we know not what purpose, there can be no assured security for the democratic governments of the world. We are now about to accept gauge of battle with this natural foe to liberty and shall, if necessary, spend the whole force of the nation to check and nullify its pretensions and its power; We are glad, now that we see the facts with no veil of false pretence about them, to fight thus for the ultimate peace of the world and for the liberation of its peoples, the German people included: for the rights of nations great and small and the privilege of men everywhere to choose their way of life and obedience. The world must be made safe for democracy. Its peace must be planted upon the tested foundations of political liberty. We must have no selfish ends to serve. We desire no conquest, no dominion. We seek no indemnities for ourselves, no material compensation for the sacrifices we shall freely make. We are but one of the champions of the rights of mankind. We shall be satisfied when these rights have been made as secure as the faith and the freedom of nations can make them...

There are, it may be, many months of fiery trial and sacrifice ahead of us. It is a fearful thing to lead this great peaceful people into war, into the most terrible and disastrous of all wars, civilization itself seeming to be in the balance. But the right is more precious than peace, and we shall fight for the things, which we have always carried nearest our hearts—for democracy, for the right of those who submit to authority to have a voice in their own governments, for the rights and liberties of small nations, for a universal dominion of right by such a consort of free peoples as shall bring peace and safety to all nations and make the world itself at last free. To such a task we can dedicate our lives and our fortunes, everything that we are and everything that we have, with the pride of those who know that the day has come when America is privileged to spend her blood and her might for the principles that gave her birth and happiness and the peace which she has treasured. God helping her, she can do no other.

Address to Congress on Declaring War against Germany, April 2, 1917.

The Right of Self-government for Peoples

The position of America in this war is so clearly avowed that no man can be excused for mistaking it. She seeks no material profit or aggrandizement of any kind. She is fighting for no advantage or selfish object of her own, but for the liberation of peoples everywhere from the aggressions of autocratic force. The ruling classes in Germany have begun of late to profess a like liberality and justice of purpose, but only to preserve the power they have set up in Germany and the selfish advantages which they have wrongly gained for themselves and their private projects of power all the way from Berlin to Baghdad and beyond. Government after Government has by their influence, without open conquest of its territory, been linked together in a net of intrigue directed against nothing less than the peace and liberty of the world. The meshes of that intrigue must be broken unless wrongs already done are undone, and adequate measures must be taken to prevent it from ever again being rewoven or repaired.

Of course, the Imperial German Government and those whom it is using for their own undoing are seeking to obtain pledges that war will end in the restoration of the status quo ante. It was the status quo ante out of which this iniquitous war issued forth, the power of the Imperial German Government within the Empire and its widespread domination and influence outside of that Empire. That status must be altered in such fashion as to prevent any such hideous thing from ever happening again.

We are fighting for the liberty, the self-government, and the undictated development of all peoples, and every feature of the settlement that concludes this war must be conceived and executed for that purpose. Wrongs must first be righted and then adequate safeguards must be created to prevent their being committed again. We ought not to consider remedies merely because they have a pleasing and sonorous sound. Practical questions can be settled only by practical means. Phrases will not accomplish the result. Effective readjustments will, and whatever readjustments are necessary must be made.

But they must follow a principle and that principle is plain. No people must be forced under sovereignty under which it does not wish to live. No territory must change hands except for the purpose of securing those who inhabit it a fair chance of life and liberty. No indemnities must be insisted on except those that constitute payment for manifest wrongs done. No readjustments of power must be made except such as will tend to secure the future peace of the world and the future welfare and happiness of its peoples.

And then the free peoples of the world must draw together in some common covenant, some genuine and practical co-operation that will in effect combine their force to secure peace and justice in the dealings of nations with one another. The brotherhood of mankind must no longer be a fair but empty phrase; it must be given a structure of force and reality. The nations must realize their common life and effect a workable partnership to secure that life against the aggressions of autocratic and self-pleasing power.

For these things we can afford to pour out blood and treasure. For these are the things we have always professed to desire, and unless we pour out blood and treasure now and succeed we may never be able to unite or show conquering force again in the great cause of human liberty. The day has come to conquer or submit. If the forces of autocracy can divide us they will overcome us; if we stand together victory is certain and the liberty which victory will secure. We can afford then to be generous, but we cannot afford then or now to be weak or omit any single guarantee of justice and security.

Cablegram to Russia. May 26, 1917.

II. America and World Service

Champion of the Rights of Man

What are we going to do with the influence and power of this great Nation? Are we going to play the old role of using that power for our own aggrandizement and material benefit only? You know what that may mean? It may upon occasion mean that we shall use it to make the peoples of other nations suffer in the way in which we said it was intolerable to suffer when we uttered our Declaration of Independence.

The Department of State at Washington is constantly called upon to back up the commercial enterprises and the industrial enterprises of the United States in foreign countries, and it at one time went so far in that direction that all its diplomacy came to be designated as "dollar diplomacy." It was called upon to support every man who wanted to earn anything anywhere if he was an American. But there ought to be a limit to that. There is no man more interested than I am in carrying the enterprise of American business men to every quarter of the globe. I was interested in it long before I was suspected of being a politician. I have been preaching it year after year as the great thing that lay is the future for the United States, to show her wit and skill and enterprise and influence in every country in the world. But observe the limit to all that which is laid upon us perhaps more than upon any other nation in the world. We set this Nation up, at any rate we professed to set it up, to vindicate the rights of men. We did not name any differences between one race and another. We did not set up any barriers against any particular people. We opened our gates to all the world and said, "Let all men who wish to be free come to us and they will be welcome." We said, "This independence of ours is not a selfish thing for our own exclusive private use. It is for everybody to whom we can find the means of extending it." We cannot with that oath taken in our youth, we cannot with that great ideal set before us when we were a young people and numbered a scant 3,000,000, take upon ourselves, now that we are 100,000,000 strong, any other conception of duty than we then entertained. If American enterprise in foreign countries, particularly in those foreign countries which are not strong enough to resist us, takes the shape of imposing upon and exploiting the mass of the people of that country it ought to be checked and not encouraged. I am willing to get anything for an American that money and enterprise can obtain except the suppression of the rights of other men. I will not help any man buy a power which he ought not to exercise over his fellow beings...

A patriotic American is a man who is not niggardly and selfish in the things that he enjoys that make for human liberty and the rights of man. He wants to share them with the whole world, and he is never so proud of the great flag under which he lives as when it comes to mean to other people as well as to himself a symbol of hope and liberty. I would be ashamed of this flag if it ever did anything outside America that we would not permit it to do inside of America.

The world is becoming more complicated every day, my fellow citizens. No man ought to be foolish enough to think that he understands it all. And, therefore, I am glad that there are some simple things in the world. One of the simple things is principle. Honesty is a perfectly simple thing. It is hard for me to believe that in most circumstances when a man has a choice of ways he does not know which is the right way and which is the wrong way. No man who has chosen the wrong way ought even to come into Independence Square; it is holy ground which he ought not to tread upon. He ought not to come where immortal voices have uttered the great sentences of such a document as this Declaration of Independence upon which rests the liberty of a whole nation...

It is very inspiring, my friends, to come to this that may be called the original fountain of independence and liberty in America and here drink draughts of patriotic feeling which seem to renew the very blood in one's veins. Down in Washington sometimes when the days are hot and the business presses intolerably and there are so many things to do that it does not seem possible to do anything in the way it ought to be done, it is always possible to lift one's thoughts above the task of the moment and, as it were, to realize that great thing of which we are all parts, the great body of American feeling and American principle. No man could do the work that has to be done in Washington if he allowed himself to be separated from that body of principle. He must make himself feel that he is a part of the people of the United States, that he is trying to think not only for them, but with them, and then he cannot feel lonely. He not only cannot feel lonely but he cannot feel afraid of anything.

My dream is that as the years go on and the world knows more and more of America it will also drink at these fountains of youth and renewal; that it also will turn to America for those moral inspirations which lie at the basis of all freedom; that the world will never fear America unless it feels that it is engaged in some enterprise which is inconsistent with the rights of humanity; and that America will come into the full light of the day when all shall know that she puts human rights above all other rights and that her flag is the flag not only of America but of humanity.

What other great people has devoted itself to this exalted ideal? To what other nation in the world can all eyes look for an instant sympathy that thrills the whole body politic when men anywhere are fighting for their rights? I do not know that there will ever be a declaration of independence and of grievances for mankind, but I believe that if any such document is ever drawn it will be drawn in the spirit of the American Declaration of Independence, and that America has lifted high the light which will shine unto all generations and guide the feet of mankind to the goal of justice and liberty and peace.

Address at Independence Hall, Philadelphia, July 4, 1914.

The Christian Basis of Service

I wonder if we attach sufficient importance to Christianity as a mere instrumentality in the life of mankind. For one, I am not fond of thinking of Christianity as the means of saving individual souls. I have always been very impatient of processes and institutions which said that their purpose was to put every man in the way of developing his character. My advice is; Do not think about your character. If you will think about what you ought to do for other people, your character will take care of itself. Character is a by-product, and any man who devotes himself to its cultivation in his own case will become a selfish prig. The only way your powers can become great is by exerting them outside the circle of your own narrow, special, selfish interests. And that is the reason of Christianity. Christ came into the world to save others, not to save Himself; and no man is a true Christian who does not think constantly of how he can lift his brother, how he can assist his friend, how he can enlighten mankind, how he can make virtue the rule of conduct in the circle in which he lives...

Life, gentlemen—the life of society, the life of the world—has constantly to be fed from the bottom. It has to be fed by those great sources of strength which are constantly rising in new generations. Red blood has to be pumped into it. New fibre has to be supplied. That is the reason I have always said that I believed in popular institutions. If you can guess beforehand whom your rulers are going to be, you can guess with a very great certainty that most of them will not be fit to rule. The beauty of popular institutions is that you do not know where the man is going to come from, and you do not care so he is the right man. You do not know whether he will come from the avenue or from the alley. You do not know whether he will come from the city or from the farm. You do not know whether you will ever have heard that name before or not. Therefore you do not limit at any point your supply of new strength. You do not say it has got to come through the blood of a particular family or through the processes of a particular training, or by anything except the native impulses and genius of the man himself. The humblest hovel, therefore, may produce you your greatest man. A very humble hovel did produce you one of your greatest men. That is the process of life, this constant surging up of the new strength of unnamed, unrecognised, uncatalogued men who are just getting into the running, who are just coming up from the masses of the unrecognised multitude. You do not know when you will see above the level masses of the crowd some great stature lifted head and shoulders above the rest, shouldering its way, not violently but gently, to the front and saying, "Here am I; follow me." And his voice will be your voice, his thought will be your thought, and you will follow him as if you were following the best things in yourselves...

Eternal vigilance is the price, not only of liberty, but of a great many other things. It is the price of everything that is good. It is the price of one's own soul. It is the price of the souls of the people you love; and when it comes down to the final reckoning you have a standard that is immutable. What shall a man give in exchange for his own soul? Will he sell that? Will he consent to see another man sell his soul? Will he consent to see the conditions of his community such that men's souls are debauched and trodden underfoot in the mire? What shall he give in exchange for his own soul, or any other man's soul? And since the world, the world of affairs, the world of society, is nothing less and nothing more than all of us put together, it is a great enterprise for the salvation of the soul in this world as well as in the next. There is a text in Scripture that has always interested me profoundly. It says godliness is profitable in this life as well as in the life that is to come; and if you do not start it in this life, it will not reach the life that is to come. Your measurements, your directions, your whole momentum, have to be established before you reach the next world. This world is intended as the place in which we shall show that we know how to grow in the stature of manliness and of righteousness...

If a man had to measure the accomplishments of society, the progress of reform, the speed of the world's betterment, by the few little things that happened in his own life, by the trifling things that he can contribute to accomplish, he would feel indeed that the cost was much greater than the result. But no man can look at the past of the history of this world without seeing a vision of the future of the history of this world: and when you think of the accumulated moral forces that have made one age better than another age in the progress of mankind, then you can open your eyes to the vision. You can see that age by age, though with a blind struggle in the dust of the road, though often mistaking the path and losing its way in the mire, mankind is yet—sometimes with bloody hands and battered knees—nevertheless struggling step after step up the slow stages to the day when he. shall live in the full light which shines upon the uplands, where all the light that illumines mankind shines direct from the face of God.

Address before the American Bar Association, October 24, 1914.

The Mission of America

Think of the deep-wrought destruction of economic resources, of life, and of hope that is taking place in some parts of the world, and think of the reservoir of hope, the reservoir of energy, the reservoir of sustenance that there is in this great land of plenty! May we not look forward to the time when we shall be called blessed among the nations, because we succoured the nations of the world in their time of distress and of dismay? I for one pray God that that solemn hour may come, and I know the solidity of character and I know the exaltation of hope, I know the big principle with which the American people will respond to the call of the world for this service. I thank God that those who believe in America, who try to serve her people, are likely to be also what America herself from the first hoped and meant to be —the servant of mankind.

Jackson Day Address at Indianapolis, January 8, 1915.

America as Mediator

We are the mediating Nation of the world. I do not mean that we undertake not to mind our own business and to mediate where other people are quarrelling. I mean the word in a broader sense. We are compounded of the nations of the world; we mediate their blood, we mediate their traditions, we mediate their sentiments, their tastes, their passions, we are ourselves compounded of those things. We. are, therefore, able to understand all nations. We are able to understand them in the compound, not separately, as partisans, but unitedly as knowing and comprehending and embodying them all. It is in that sense that I mean that America is a mediating Nation. The opinion of America, the action of America, is ready to turn, and free to turn, in any direction. Did you ever reflect upon how almost every other nation has through long centuries been headed in one direction? That is not true of the United States. The United States has no racial momentum. It has no history back of it which makes it run all its energies and all its ambitions in one particular direction. And America is particularly free in this, that she has no hampering ambitions as a world power. We do not want a foot of anybody's territory. If we have been obliged by circumstances, or considered ourselves to be obliged by circumstances, in the past, to take territory which we otherwise would not have thought of taking, I believe I am right in saying that we have considered it our duty to administer that territory, not for ourselves but for the people living in it, and to put this burden upon our consciences—not to think that this thing is ours for our use, but to regard ourselves as trustees of the great business for those to whom it does really belong, trustees ready to hand it over to the *cestui que* trust at any time when the business seems to make that possible and feasible. That is what I mean by saying that we have no hampering ambitions. We do not want anything that does not belong to us. Is not a nation in that position free to serve other nations, and is not a nation like that ready to form some part of the assessing opinion of the world?

Address at a Meeting of the Associated Press at New York, April 20, 1915.

Ideals of American Citizenship

This is the only country in the world which experiences this constant and repeated rebirth. Other countries depend upon the multiplication of their own native people. This country is constantly drinking strength out of new sources by the voluntary association with it of great bodies of strong men and forward-looking women out of other lands. And so by the gift of the free will of independent people it is being constantly renewed from generation to generation by the same process by which it was originally created. It is as if humanity had determined to see to it that this great Nation, founded for the benefit of humanity, should not lack the allegiance of the people of the world.

You have just taken an oath of allegiance to the United States. Of allegiance to whom? Of allegiance to no one, unless it be to God—certainly not of allegiance to those who temporarily represent this great Government. You have taken an oath of allegiance to a great ideal, to a great body of principles, to a great hope of the human race... And while you bring all countries with you, you come with a purpose of leaving all other countries behind you—bringing what is best of their spirit, but not looking over your shoulders and seeking to perpetuate what you intended to leave behind in them. I certainly would not be one even to suggest that a man cease to love the home of his birth and the nation of his origin— these things are very sacred and ought not to be put out of our hearts—but it is one thing to love the place where you were born and it is another thing to dedicate yourself to the place which you go. You cannot dedicate yourself to America unless you become in every respect and with every purpose of your will thorough Americans. You can not become Americans if you think of yourselves in groups. America does not consist of groups. A man who thinks of himself as belonging to a particular national group in America has not yet become an American, and the man who goes among you to trade upon your nationality is no worthy son to live under the Stars and Stripes.

My urgent advice to you would be, not only always to think first of America, but always, also, to think first of humanity. You do not love humanity if you seek to divide humanity into jealous camps. Humanity can be welded together only by love, by sympathy, by justice, not by jealousy and hatred. I am sorry for the man who seeks to make personal capital out of the passions of his fellow-men. He has lost the touch and ideal of America, for America was created to unite mankind by those passions which lift and not by the passions which separate and debase. We came to America, either ourselves or in the persons of our ancestors, to better the ideals of men, to make them see finer things than they had seen before, to get rid of the things that divide and to make sure of the things that unite. It was but an historical accident no doubt that this great country was called the "United States" yet I am very thankful that it has that word "United" in its title, and the man who seeks to divide man from man, group from group, interest from interest in this great Union is striking at its very heart.

It is a very interesting circumstance to me, in thinking of those of you who have sworn allegiance to this great Government, that you were drawn across the ocean by some beckoning finger of hope, by some belief, by some vision of a new kind of justice, by some expectation of a better kind of life. No doubt you have been disappointed in some of us. Some of us are very disappointing. No doubt you have found that justice in the United States goes only with a pure heart and a right purpose as it does everywhere else in the world. No doubt what you found here did not seem touched for you, after all, with the complete beauty of the ideal which you had conceived beforehand. But remember this: If we had grown at all poor in the ideal, you brought some of it with you. A man does not go out to seek the thing that is not in him. A man does not hope for the thing he does not believe in, and if some of us have forgotten what America believed in, you, at any rate, imported in your own hearts a renewal of the belief. That is the reason that I, for one, make you welcome. If I have in any degree forgotten what America was intended for, I will thank God if you will remind me. I was born in America. You dreamed dreams of what America was to be, and I hope you brought the dreams with you. No man that does not see visions will ever realize any high hope or undertake any high enterprise. Just because you brought dreams with you America is more likely to realise dreams such as you brought. You are enriching us if you came expecting us to be better than we are.

See, my friends, what that means. It means that Americans must have a consciousness different from the consciousness of every other nation in the world. I am not saying this with even the slightest thought of criticism of other nations. You know how it is with a family. A family gets centred on itself if it is not careful and is less interested in the neighbours than it is in its own members. So a nation that is not constantly renewed out of new sources is apt to have the narrowness and prejudice of a family; whereas, America must have this consciousness, that on all sides it touches elbows and touches hearts with all the nations of mankind. The example of America must be a special example. The example of America must be the example not merely of peace because it will not fight, but of peace because peace is the healing and elevating influence of the world and strife is not. There is such a thing as a man being too proud to fight. There is such a thing as a nation being so right that it does not need to convince others by force that it is right.

You have come into this great Nation voluntarily seeking something that we have to give, and all that we have to give is this: We cannot exempt you from work. No man is exempt from work anywhere in the world. We cannot exempt you from the strife and the heartbreaking burden of struggle of the day—that is common of mankind everywhere; we cannot exempt you from the loads that you must carry. We can only make them light by the spirit in which they are carried. That is the spirit of hope, it is the spirit of liberty, it is the spirit of justice.

Address to Naturalized Citizens at Convention Hall, Philadelphia, May 10, 1915.

Isolationism at the End

The world will never be again what it has been. The United States will never be again what it has been. The United States was once in enjoyment of what we used to call splendid isolation. The three thousand miles of the Atlantic seemed to hold all European affairs at arm's length from us. The great spaces of the Pacific seemed to disclose no threat of influence upon our politics.

Now, from across the Atlantic and from across the Pacific we feel to the quick the influences which are affecting ourselves... We can determine to a large extent who is to be financed and who is not to be financed. That is the reason I say that the United States will never be again what it has been. So it does not suffice to look, as some gentlemen are looking, back over their shoulders, to suggest that we do again what we did when we were provincial and isolated and unconnected with the great forces of the world, for now we are in the great drift of humanity which is to determine the politics of every country in the world.

With this outlook, is it worthwhile to stop to think of party advantage? Is it worth stopping to think of how we have voted in the past? We are now going to vote, if we be men with eyes open that can see the world, as those who wish to make a new America in a new world mean the same old thing for mankind that it meant when this great Republic was set up; mean hope and justice and righteous judgment and unselfish action. Why, my fellow-citizens, it is an unprecedented thing in the world that any nation in determining its foreign relations should be unselfish, and my ambition is to see America set the great example; not only a great example morally, but a great example intellectually... In the days to come men will no longer wonder how America is going to work out her destiny, for she will have proclaimed to them that her destiny is not divided from the destiny of the world; that her purpose is justice and love of mankind.

Address at Shadow Lawn. November 4. 1916.

III. War and Peace Aims

Definition of Peace Terms

The President suggests that an early occasion be sought to call out from all the nations now at war such an avowal of their respective views as to the terms upon which the war might be concluded and the arrangements which would be deemed satisfactory as a guarantee against its renewal or the kindling of similar conflict in the future as would make it possible frankly to. compare them. He is indifferent as to the means taken to accomplish this. He would be happy himself to serve, or even to take the initiative in its accomplishment, in any way that might prove acceptable, but he has no desire to determine the method or the instrumentality. One way will be as acceptable to him as another if only the great object he has in mind be attained.

He takes the liberty of calling attention to the fact that the objects which the statesmen of the belligerents on both sides have in mind in this war are virtually the same, as stated in general terms to their own people and to the world. Each side desires to make the rights and privileges of weak peoples and small states as secure against aggression or denial in the future as the rights and privileges of the great and powerful states now at war. Each wishes itself to be made secure in the future, along with all other nations and peoples, against the recurrence of wars like this, and against aggression or selfish interference of any kind. Each would be jealous of the formation of any more rival leagues to preserve an uncertain balance of power amidst multiplying suspicions; but each is ready to consider the formation of a league of nations to insure peace and justice throughout the world. Before that final step can be taken, however, each deems it necessary first to settle the issues of the present war upon terms which will certainly safeguard the independence, the territorial integrity, and the political and commercial freedom of the nations involved.

In the measures to be taken to secure the future peace of the world the people and Government of the United States are as vitally and as directly interested as the Governments now at war. Their interest, moreover, in the means to be adopted to relieve the smaller and weaker peoples of the world of the peril of wrong, and violence is as quick and ardent as that of any other people or Government. They stand ready, and even eager, to co-operate in the accomplishment of these ends, when the war is over, with every influence and resource at their command. But the war must first be concluded. The terms upon which it is to be concluded they are not at liberty to suggest; but the President does feel that it is his right and his duty to point out their intimate interest in its conclusion, lest it should presently be too late to accomplish the greater things which lie beyond its conclusion, lest the situation of neutral nations, now exceedingly hard to endure, be rendered altogether intolerable, and lest, more than all, an injury be done to civilization itself which can never be atoned for or repaired.

The President therefore feels altogether justified in suggesting an immediate opportunity for a comparison of views as to the terms which must precede those ultimate arrangements for the peace of the world, which all desire and in which the neutral nations as well as those at war are ready to play their full responsible part. If the contest must continue to proceed towards undefined ends by slow attrition until the one group of belligerents or the other is exhausted, if millions after millions of human lives must continue to be offered up until on the one side or the other there are no more to offer, if resentments must be kindled that can never cool and despairs engendered from which there can be no recovery, hopes of peace and of the willing concert of free peoples will be rendered vain and idle.

The life of the entire world has been profoundly affected. Every part of the great family of mankind has felt the burden and terror of this unprecedented contest of arms. No nation in the civilized world can be said in truth to stand outside its influence or to be safe against its disturbing effects. And yet the concrete objects for which it is being waged have never been definitively stated.

The leaders of the several belligerents have, as has been said, stated those objects in general terms. But, stated in general terms, they seem the same on both sides. Never yet have the authoritative spokesmen of either side avowed the precise objects which would, if attained, satisfy them and their people that the war had been fought out. The world has been left to conjecture what definitive results, what actual exchange of guarantees, what political or territorial changes or readjustments, what stage of military success even, would bring the war to an end.

It may be that peace is nearer than we know: that the terms which the belligerents on the one side and on the other would deem it necessary to insist upon are not so irreconcilable as some have feared: that an interchange of views would clear the way at least for conference and make the permanent concord of the nations a hope of the immediate future, a concert of nations immediately practicable.

The President is not proposing peace: he is not even offering mediation. He is merely proposing that soundings be taken in order that we may learn, the neutral nations with the belligerent, how near the haven of peace may be for which all mankind longs with an intense and increasing longing. He believes that the spirit in which he speaks and the objects which he seeks will be understood by all concerned, and confidently hopes for a response which will bring a new light into the affairs of the world.

Despatch Partly in Reply to German Proposition of Peace, through Secretary Lansing, December 18, 1916.

A Concert of Nations

On the eighteenth of December last I addressed an identical note to the governments of the nations now at war requesting them to state, more definitely than they had yet been stated by either group of belligerents, the terms upon which they would deem it possible to make peace. I spoke on behalf of humanity and of the rights of all neutral nations like our own, many of whose most vital interests the war puts in constant jeopardy. The Central Powers united in a reply which stated merely that they were ready to meet their antagonists in conference to discuss terms of peace. The Entente Powers have replied much more definitely and have stated in general terms, indeed, but with sufficient definiteness to imply details, the arrangements, guarantees, and acts of reparation which they deem to be the indispensable conditions of a satisfactory settlement. We arc that much nearer a definite discussion of the peace which shall end the present war. We are that much nearer the discussion of the international concert which must thereafter hold the world at peace. In every discussion of the peace that must end this war it is taken for granted that that peace must be followed by some definite concert of power which will make it virtually impossible that any such catastrophe should ever overwhelm us again. Every lover of mankind, every sane and thoughtful man must take that for granted.

I have sought this opportunity to address you because I thought that I owed it to you, as the council associated with me in the final determination of our international obligations, to disclose to you without reserve the thought and purpose that have been taking form in my mind in regard to the duty of our Government in the days to come when it will be necessary to lay afresh and upon a new plan the foundations of peace among the nations.

It is inconceivable that the people of the United States should play no part in that great enterprise. To take part in such a service will be the opportunity for which they have sought to prepare themselves by the very principles and purposes of their polity and the approved practices of their Government ever since the days when they set up a new nation in the high and honourable hope that it might in all that it was and did show mankind the way of liberty. They cannot in honour withhold the service to which they are now about to be challenged. They do not wish to withhold it. But they owe it to themselves and to the other nations of the world to state the conditions under which they will feel free to render it.

That service is nothing less than this, to add their authority and their power to the authority and force of other nations to guarantee peace and justice throughout the world. Such a settlement cannot now be long postponed. It is right that before it comes this Government should frankly formulate the conditions upon which it would feel justified in asking our people to approve its formal and solemn adherence to a League for Peace. I am here to attempt to state those conditions.

The present war must first be ended; but we owe it to candour and to a just regard for the opinion of mankind to say that, so far as our participation in guarantees of future peace is considered, it makes a great deal of difference in what way and upon what terms it is ended. The treaties and agreements which bring it to an end must embody terms which will create a peace that is worth guaranteeing and preserving, a peace that will win the approval of mankind, not merely a peace that will serve the several interests, and immediate aims of the nations engaged. We shall have no voice in determining what those terms shall be, but we shall, I feel sure, have a voice in determining whether they shall be made lasting or not by the guarantees of a universal covenant; and our judgment upon what is fundamental and essential as a condition precedent to permanency should be spoken now, not afterwards when it may be too late.

No covenant of co-operative peace that does not include the peoples of the New World can suffice to keep the future safe against war; and yet there is only one sort of peace that the peoples of America could join in guaranteeing. The elements of that peace must be elements that engage the confidence and satisfy the principles of the American governments, elements consistent with their political faith and with the practical convictions which the peoples of America have once for all embraced and undertaken to defend.

I do not mean to say that any American government would throw any obstacle in the way of any terms of peace the governments now at war might agree upon, or seek to upset them when made, whatever they might be. I only take it for granted that mere terms of peace between the belligerents will not satisfy even the belligerents themselves. Mere agreements may not make peace secure. It will be absolutely necessary that a force be created as a guarantor of the permanency of the settlement so much greater than the force of any nation now engaged or any alliance hitherto formed or projected that no nation, no probable combination of nations could face or withstand it. If the peace presently to be made is to endure, it must be a peace made secure by the organized major force of mankind.

The terms of the immediate peace agreed upon will determine whether it is a peace for which such a guarantee can be secured. The question upon which the whole future peace and policy of the world depends is this; Is the present war a struggle for a just and secure peace, or only for a new balance of power? If it be only a struggle for a new balance of power, who will guarantee, who can guarantee, the stable equilibrium of the new arrangement? Only a tranquil Europe can be a stable Europe. There must be, not a balance of power, but a community of power; not organized rivalries, but an organized common peace.

Fortunately we have received very explicit assurances on this point. The statesmen of both of the groups of nations now arrayed against one another have said, in terms that could not be misinterpreted, that it was no part of the purpose they had in mind to crush their antagonists. But the implications of these assurances may not be equally clear to all, may not be the same on both sides of the water. I think it will be serviceable if I attempt to set forth what we understand them to be.

They imply, first of all, that it must be a peace without victory. It is not pleasant to say this. I beg that I may be permitted to put my own interpretation upon it and that it may be understood that no other interpretation was in my thought. I am seeking only to face realities and to face them without soft concealments. Victory would mean peace forced upon the loser, a victor's terms imposed upon the vanquished. It would be accepted in humiliation, under duress, at an intolerable sacrifice, and would leave a sting, a resentment, a bitter memory upon which terms of peace would rest, not permanently, but only as upon quicksand. Only a peace between equals can last. Only a peace the very principle of which is equality and a common participation in a common benefit. The right state of mind, the right feeling between nations, is as necessary for a lasting peace as is the just settlement of vexed questions of territory or of racial and national allegiance.

The equality of nations upon which peace must be founded if it is to last must be an equality of rights; the guarantees exchanged must neither recognize nor imply a difference between big nations and small, between those that are powerful and those that are weak. Right must be based upon the common strength, not upon the individual strength, of the nations upon whoso concert peace will depend. Equality of territory or of resources there of course cannot be; nor any other sort of equality not gained in the ordinary peaceful and legitimate development of the peoples themselves. But no one asks or expects anything more than an equality of rights. Mankind is looking now for freedom of life, not for equipoises of power.

And there is a deeper thing involved than even equality of right among organized nations. No peace can last, or ought to last, which does not recognize and accept the principle that governments derive all their just powers from the consent of the governed, and that no right anywhere exists to hand peoples about from sovereignty to sovereignty as if they were property. I take it for granted, for instance, if I may venture upon a single example, that statesmen everywhere are agreed that there should be a united, independent and autonomous Poland, and that henceforth inviolable security of life, worship, and of industrial and social development should be guaranteed to all peoples who have lived hitherto under the power of governments devoted to a faith and purpose hostile to their own.

I speak of this, not because of any desire to exalt an abstract political principle which has always been held very dear by those who have sought to build up liberty in America, but for the same reason that I have spoken of the other conditions of peace which seem to me clearly indispensable, because I wish frankly to uncover realities. Any peace which does not recognize and accept this principle will inevitably be upset. It will not rest upon the affections or the convictions of mankind. The ferment of spirit of whole populations will fight subtly and constantly against it, and all the world will sympathize. The world can be at peace only if its life is stable, and there can be no stability where the will is in rebellion, where there is no tranquility of spirit and a sense of justice, of freedom, and of right.

So far as practicable, moreover, every great people now struggling towards a full development of its resources and of its powers should be assured of a direct outlet to the great highways of the sea. Where this cannot be done by the cession of territory, it can no doubt be done by the neutralization of direct rights of way under the general guarantcc which will assure the peace itself. With a right comity of arrangement no nation need be shut away from free access to the open paths of the world's commerce.

And the paths of the sea must alike in law and in fact be free. The freedom of the seas is the *sine qua non* of peace, equality and co-operation. No doubt a somewhat radical reconsideration of many of the rules of international practice hitherto thought to be established may be necessary in order to make the seas indeed free and common in practically all circumstances for the use of mankind, but the motive for such changes is convincing and compelling. There can be no trust or intimacy between the peoples of the world without them. The free, constant, unthreatened intercourse of nations is an essential part of the process of peace and of development. It need not be difficult either to define or to secure the freedom of the seas if the governments of the world sincerely desire to come to an agreement concerning it.

It is a problem closely connected with the limitation of naval armaments and the co-operation of the navies of the world in keeping the seas at once free and safe. And the question of limiting naval armaments opens the wider and perhaps more difficult question of the limitation of armies and of all programmes of military preparation. Difficult and delicate as these questions are, they must be faced with the utmost candour and decided in a spirit of real accommodation if peace is to come with healing in its wings, and come to stay. Peace cannot be had without concession and sacrifice. There can be no sense of safety and equality among the nations if great preponderating armaments are henceforth to continue here and there to be built up and maintained. The statesmen of the world must plan for peace and nations must adjust and accommodate their policy to it as they have planned for war and made ready for pitiless contest and rivalry. The question of armaments, whether on land or sea, is the most immediately and intensely practical question connected with the future fortunes of nations and of mankind.

I have spoken upon these great matters without reserve and with the utmost explicitness because it has seemed to me to be necessary if the world's yearning desire for peace was anywhere to find free voice and utterance. Perhaps I am the only person in high authority amongst all the peoples of the world who is at liberty to speak and hold nothing back. I am speaking as an individual, and yet I am speaking also, of course, as the responsible head of a great government, and I feel confident that I have said what the people of the United States would wish me to say. May I not add that I hope and believe that I am in effect speaking for liberals and friends of humanity in every nation and of every programme of liberty? I would fain believe that I am speaking for the silent mass of mankind everywhere who have as yet had no place of opportunity to speak their real hearts out concerning the death and ruin they see to have come already upon the persons and the homes they hold most dear.

And in holding out the expectation that the people and Government of the United States will join the other civilized nations of the world in guaranteeing the permanence of peace upon such terms as I have named I speak with the greater boldness and confidence because it is clear to every man who can think that there is in this promise no breach in either our traditions or our policy as a nation, but a fulfilment, rather, of all that we have professed or striven for.

I am proposing, as it were, that the nations should with one accord adopt the doctrine of President Monroe as the doctrine of the world: that no nation should seek to extend its polity over any other nation or people, but that every people should be left free to determine its own polity, its own way of development, unhindered, unthreatened, unafraid, the little along with the great and powerful.

I am proposing that all nations henceforth avoid entangling alliances which would draw them into competitions of power, catch them in a net of intrigue and selfish rivalry, and disturb their own affairs with influences intruded from without. There is no entangling alliance in a concert of power. When all unite to act in the same sense and with the same purpose all act in a common interest and are free to live their own lives under a common protection.

I am proposing government by the consent of the governed; that freedom of the seas which in international conference after conference representatives of the United States have urged with the eloquence of those who are the convinced disciples of liberty; and that moderation of armaments which makes armies and navies a power for order merely, not an instrument of aggression or of selfish violence.

These are American principles, American policies. We could stand for no others. And they are also the principles and policies of forward looking men and women everywhere, of every modern nation, of every enlightened community. They are the principles of mankind and must prevail.

Address to the Senate. January 22. 1917. Text in Full.

German Militarism must Cease

Is it not easy to understand the eagerness for peace that has been manifested from Berlin ever since the snare was set and sprung? Peace, peace, peace has been the talk of her Foreign Office for now a year and more; not peace upon her own initiative, but upon the initiative of the nations over which she now deems herself to hold the advantage. A little of the talk has been public, but most of it has been private. Through all sorts of channels it has come to me, and in all sorts of guises, but never with the terms disclosed which the German Government would be willing to accept. That government has other valuable pawns in its hands besides those that I have mentioned. It still holds a valuable part of France, though with slowly relaxing grasp, and practically the whole of Belgium. Its armies press close upon Russia and overrun Poland at their will. It cannot go further; it dare not go back. It wishes to close its bargain before it is too late and it has little left to offer for the pound of flesh it will demand.

The military masters under whom Germany is bleeding see very clearly to what point Fate has brought them. If they fall back or are forced back an inch, their power both abroad and at home will fall to pieces like a house of cards. It is their power at home they are thinking about now more than their power abroad. It is that power which is trembling under their very feet; and deep fear has entered their hearts. They have but one chance to perpetuate their military power or even their controlling political influence. If they can secure peace now with the immense advantages still in their hands which they have up to this point apparently gained, they will have justified themselves before the German people; they will have gained by force what they promised to gain by it: an immense expansion of German power, an immense enlargement of German industrial and commercial opportunities. Their prestige will be secure, and with their prestige their political power. If they fail, their people will thrust them aside; a government accountable to the people themselves will be set up in Germany as it has been in England, in the United States, in France, and in all the great countries of the modern time except Germany. If they succeed they are safe and Germany and the world are undone; if they fail Germany is saved and the world will be at peace. If they succeed, America will fall within the menace. We and all the rest of the world must remain armed, as they will remain, and must make ready for the next step in their aggression; if they fail, the world may unite for peace and Germany may be of the union.

Do you not now understand the new intrigue, the intrigue for peace, and why the masters of Germany do not hesitate to use any agency that promises to effect their purpose, the deceit of the nations? Their present particular aim is to deceive all those who throughout the world stand for the rights of peoples and the self-government of nations; for they see what immense strength the forces of justice and of liberalism are gathering out of this war. They are employing liberals in their enterprise.

They are using men, in Germany and without, as their spokesmen whom they have hitherto despised and oppressed, using them for their own destruction, socialists, the leaders of labour, the thinkers they have hitherto sought to silence. Let them once succeed and these men, now their tools, will be ground to powder beneath the weight of the great military empire they will have set up; the revolutionists in Russia will be cut off from all succour or co-operation in western Europe and a counter revolution fostered and supported; Germany herself will lose her chance of freedom: and all Europe will arm for the next, the final struggle.

The sinister intrigue is being no less actively conducted in this country than in Russia and in every country in Europe to which the agents and dupes of the Imperial German Government can get access. That government has many spokesmen here, in places high and low. They have learned discretion. They keep within the law. It is opinion they utter now, not sedition. They proclaim the liberal purposes of their masters; declare this a foreign war which can touch America with no danger to either her lands or her institutions; set England at the centre of the stage and talk of her ambition to assert economic dominion throughout the world; appeal to our ancient tradition of isolation in the politics of the nations; and seek to undermine the government with false professions of loyalty to its principles.

But they will make no headway. The false betray themselves always in every accent. It is only friends and partisans of the German Government whom we have already identified who utter these thinly disguised disloyalties. The facts are patent to all the world, and nowhere are they more plainly seen than in the United States, where we are accustomed to deal with facts and not with sophistries; and the great fact that stands out above all the rest is that this is a Peoples' War, a war for freedom and justice arid self-government amongst all the nations of the world, a war to make the world safe for the peoples who live upon it and have made it their own, the German people themselves included; and that with us rests the choice to break through all these hypocrisies and patent cheats and masks of brute force and help set the world free, or else stand aside and let it be dominated a long age through by sheer weight of arms and the arbitrary choices of self-constituted masters, by the nation which can maintain the biggest armies and the most irresistible armaments, a power to which the world has afforded no parallel and in the face of which political freedom must wither and perish.

For us there is but one choice. We have made it. Woe be to the man or group of men that seeks to stand in our way in this day of high resolution when every principle we hold dearest is to be vindicated and made secure for the salvation of the nations. We arc ready to plead at the bar of history, and our flag shall wear a new lustre. Once more we shall make good with our lives and fortunes the great faith to which we were born, and a new glory shall shine in the face of our people.

Address on Flag Day at Washington. June 14, 1917.

Papal Peace Proposals

In acknowledgment of the communication of Your Holiness to the belligerent peoples, dated August 1, 1917, the President of the United States requests me to transmit the following reply:

Every heart that has not been blinded and hardened by his terrible war must be touched by this moving appeal of His Holiness the Pope, must feel the dignity and force of the humane and generous motives which prompted it, and must fervently wish that we might take the path of peace he so persuasively points out. But it would be folly to take it if it does not in fact lead to the goal he proposes. Our response must be based upon the stem facts and upon nothing else. It is not a mere cessation of arms he desires; it is a stable and enduring peace. This agony must not be gone through with again, and it must be a matter of very sober judgment what will insure against it.

His Holiness in substance proposes that we return to the *status quo ante bellum*, and that then there be a general condonation, disarmament, and a concert of nations based upon an acceptance of the principle of arbitration; that by a similar concert freedom of the seas be established; and that the territorial claims of France and Italy, the perplexing problems of the Balkan States, and the restitution of Poland be left to such conciliatory adjustments as may be possible in the new temper of such a peace, due regard being paid to the aspirations of the peoples whose political fortunes and affiliations will be involved.

It is manifest that no part of this programme can be successfully carried out unless the restitution of the *status quo ante* furnishes a firm and satisfactory basis for it. The object of this war is to deliver the free peoples of the world from the menace of the actual power of a vast military establishment controlled by an irresponsible government which, having secretly planned to dominate the world, proceeded to carry the plan out without regard either to the sacred obligations of treaty or the long-established practices and long-cherished principles of international action and honour; which chose its own time for the war; delivered its blow fiercely and suddenly; stopped at no barrier either of law or of mercy; swept a whole continent with the tide of blood—not the blood of soldiers only, but the blood of innocent women and children also and of the helpless poor; and now stands balked but not defeated, the enemy of four-fifths of the world. The power is not the German people. It is the ruthless master of the German people. It is no business of ours how that great people came under its control or submitted with temporary zest to the domination of its purpose; but it is our business to see to it that the history of the rest of the world is no longer left to its handling.

To deal with such a power by way of peace upon the plan proposed by His Holiness the Pope would, so far as we can see, involve a recuperation of its strength and a renewal of its policy; would make it necessary to create a permanent hostile combination of nations against the German people who are its instruments; and would result in abandoning the newborn Russia to the intrigue, the manifold subtle interference, and the certain counter-revolution which would be attempted by all the malign influences to which the German Government has of late accustomed the world. Can peace be based upon a restitution of its power or upon any word of honour it could pledge in a treaty of settlement and accommodation?

Responsible statesmen must now everywhere see, if they never saw before, that no peace can rest securely upon political or economic restrictions meant to benefit some nations and cripple or embarrass others, upon vindictive action of any sort, or any kind of revenge or deliberate injury. The American people have suffered intolerable wrongs at the hands of the Imperial German Government, but they desire no reprisal upon the German people who have themselves suffered all things in this war which they did not choose. They believe that peace should rest upon the rights of peoples, not the rights of Governments—the rights of peoples great or small, weak or powerful—their equal right to freedom and security and self-government and to a participation upon fair terms in the economic opportunities of the world, the German people of course included if they will accept equality and not seek domination.

The test, therefore, of every plan of peace is this: Is it based upon the faith of all the peoples involved or merely upon the word of an ambitious and intriguing government on the one hand and of a group of free peoples on the other? This is a test which goes to the root of the matter and it is the test which must be applied.

The purposes of the United States in this war are known to the whole world, to every people to whom the truth has been permitted to come. They do not need to be stated again. We seek no material advantage of any kind. We believe that the intolerable wrongs done in this war by the furious and brutal power of the Imperial German Government ought to be repaired, but not at the expense of the sovereignty of any people—rather a vindication of the sovereignty both of those that are weak and of those that are strong. Punitive damages, the dismemberment of empires, the establishment of selfish and exclusive economic leagues, we deem inexpedient and in the end worse than futile, no proper basis for a peace of any kind, least of all for an enduring peace. That must be based upon justice and fairness and the common rights of mankind.

We cannot take the word of the present rulers of Germany as a guarantee of anything that is to endure, unless explicitly supported by such conclusive evidence of the will and purpose of the German people themselves as the other peoples of the world would be justified in accepting. Without such guarantees treaties of settlement, agreements for disarmament, covenants to set up arbitration in the place of force, territorial adjustments, reconstitutions of small nations, if made with the German

Government, no man, no nation could now depend on. We must await some new evidence of the purposes of the great peoples of the Central Powers. God grant it may be given soon and in a way to restore the confidence of all peoples everywhere in the faith of nations and the possibility of a covenanted peace.

Reply to the Pope through Secretary Lancing. August 27, 1917.

Free Germany must Speak

A Thing without conscience or honour or capacity for covenanted peace must be crushed and, if it be not utterly brought to an end, at least shut out from the friendly intercourse of the nations; and, second, that when this Thing and its power are indeed defeated and the time comes that we can discuss peace—when the German people have spokesmen whose word we can believe and when those spokesmen are ready in the name of their people to accept the common judgment of the nations as to what shall henceforth be the bases of law and of covenant for the life of the world—we shall be willing and glad to pay the full price for peace, and pay it ungrudgingly. We know what that price will be. It will be full, impartial justice—justice done at every point and to every nation that the final settlement must affect, our enemies as well as our friends.

You catch, with me, the voices of humanity that are in the air. They grow daily more audible, more articulate, more persuasive, and they come from the hearts of men everywhere. They insist that the war shall not end in vindictive action of any kind; that no nation or people shall be robbed or punished because the irresponsible rulers of a single country have themselves done deep and abominable wrong. It is this thought that has been expressed in the formula, "No annexations, no contributions, no punitive indemnities." Just because this crude formula expresses the instinctive judgment as to right of plain men everywhere it has been made diligent use of by the masters of German intrigue to lead the people of Russia astray—and the people of every other country their agents could reach, in order that a premature peace might be brought about before autocracy has been taught its final and convincing lesson, and the people of the world put in control of their own destinies.

But the fact that a wrong use has been made of a just idea is no reason why a right use should not be made of it. It ought to be brought under the patronage of its real friends. Let it be said again that autocracy must first be shown the utter futility of its claims to power or leadership in the modem world. It is impossible to apply any standard of justice so long as such forces are unchecked and undefeated as the present masters of Germany command. Not until that has been done can Right be set up as arbiter and peacemaker among the nations. But when that has been done—as, God willing, it assuredly will be —we must at last be free to do an unprecedented thing, and this is the time to avow our purpose to do it. We shall be free to base peace on generosity and justice, to the exclusion of all selfish claims to advantage on the part of the victors.

Let there be no misunderstanding, our present and immediate task is to win the war, and nothing shall turn us aside from it until it is accomplished. Every power and resource we possess, whether of men, of money, or of materials, is being devoted and will continue to be devoted to that purpose until it is achieved. Those who desire to bring peace about before that purpose is achieved I counsel to carry their advice elsewhere. We will not entertain it. We shall regard the war as won only when the German people say to us, through properly accredited representatives, that they are ready to agree to a settlement based upon justice and the reparation of the wrongs their rulers have done...

The people of Germany are being told by the men whom they now permit to deceive them and to act as their masters that they are fighting for the very life and existence of their Empire, a war of desperate self-defence against deliberate aggression. Nothing could be more grossly or wantonly false, and we must seek by the utmost openness and candour as to our real aims to convince them of its falseness. We are in fact fighting for their emancipation from fear, along with our own—from the fear as well as from the fact of unjust attack by neighbours or rivals or schemers after world empire. No one is threatening the existence or the independence or the peaceful enterprise of the German Empire.

The worst that can happen to the detriment of the German people is this, that if they should still, after the war is over, continue to be obliged to live under ambitious and intriguing masters interested to disturb the peace of the world, men or classes of men whom the other peoples of the world could not trust, it might be impossible to admit them to the partnership of nations which must henceforth guarantee the world's peace. That partnership must be a partnership of peoples, not a mere partnership of governments. It might be impossible, also, in such untoward circumstances, to admit Germany to the free economic intercourse which must inevitably spring out of the other partnerships of a real peace. But there would be no aggression in that; and such a situation, inevitable because of distrust, would in the very nature of things sooner or later cure itself, by processes which would assuredly set in.

The wrongs, the very deep wrongs, committed in this war will have to be righted. That of course. But they cannot and must not be righted by the commission of similar wrongs against Germany and her allies. The world will not permit the commission of similar wrongs as a means of reparation and settlement. Statesmen must by this time have learned that the opinion of the world is everywhere wide awake and fully comprehends the issues' involved. No representative of any self-governed nation will dare disregard it by attempting any such covenants of selfishness and compromise as were entered into at the Congress of Vienna. The thought of the plain people here and everywhere throughout the world, the people who enjoy no privilege and have very simple and unsophisticated standards of right and wrong, is the air all governments must henceforth breathe if they would live. It is in the full disclosing light of that thought that all policies must be conceived and executed in this mid-day hour of the world's life. German rulers have been able to upset the peace of the world only because the German people were not suffered under their tutelage to share the comradeship of the other peoples of the world in thought or in purpose. They were allowed to have no opinion of their own which might be set up as a rule of conduct for those who exercised authority over them. But the congress that concludes this war will feel the full strength of the tides that run now in the hearts and con-sciences of free men everywhere. Its conclusions will run with those tides.

Address to Congress, December 4, 1917.

The Fourteen Points

There is no confusion of counsel among the adversaries of the Central Powers, no uncertainty of principle, no vagueness of detail. The only secrecy of counsel, the only lack of fearless frankness, the only failure to make defin-ite statement of the objects of the war, lies with Germany and her Allies. The issues of life and death hang upon these definitions. No statesman who has the least con-ception of his responsibility ought for a moment to per-mit himself to continue this tragical and appalling outpouring of blood and treasure unless he is sure bey-ond a peradventure that the objects of the vital sacrifice are part and parcel of the very life of Society and that the people for whom he speaks think them right and imperative as he does.

There is, moreover, a voice calling for these definitions of principle and of purpose which is, it seems to me, more thrilling and more compelling than any of the many moving voices with which the troubled air of the world is filled. It is the voice of the Russian people. They are prostrate and all but helpless, it would seem, before the grim power of Germany, which has hitherto known no relenting and no pity. Their power, apparently, is shattered. And yet their soul is not subservient. They will not yield either in principle or in action. Their conception of what is right, of what is humane and honourable for them to accept, has been stated with a frankness, a largeness of view, a generosity of spirit, and a universal human sympathy which must challenge the admiration of every friend of mankind; and they have refused to compound their ideals or desert others that they themselves may be safe. They call to us to say what it is that we desire, in what, if in anything, our purpose and our spirit differ from theirs; and I believe that the people of the United States would wish me to respond, with utter simplicity and frankness. Whether their present leaders believe it or not, it is our heartfelt desire and hope that some way may be opened whereby we may be privileged to assist the people of Russia to attain their utmost hope of liberty and ordered peace.

It will be our wish and purpose that the processes of peace, when they are begun, shall be absolutely open and that they shall involve and permit henceforth no secret understandings of any kind. The day of conquest and aggrandizement is gone by; so is also the day of secret covenants entered into in the interest of particular governments and likely at some unlooked-for moment to upset the peace of the world. It is this happy fact, now clear to the view of every public man whose thoughts do not still linger in an age that is dead and, gone, which makes it possible for every nation whose purposes are consistent with justice and the peace of the world to avow now or at any time the objects it has in view.

We entered this war because violations of right had occurred which touched us to the quick and made the life of our own people impossible unless they were corrected and the world secured once for all against their recurrence. What we demand in this war, therefore, is nothing peculiar to ourselves. It is that the world be made fit and safe to live in; and particularly that it be made safe for every peace-loving nation which, like our own, wishes to live its own life, determine its own institutions, be assured of justice and fair dealing by the other peoples of the world as against force and selfish aggression. All the peoples of the world are in effect partners in this interest, and for our own part we see very clearly that unless justice be done to others it will not be done to us. The programme of the world's peace, therefore, is our programme; and that programme, the only possible programme, as we see it, is this:

I.   Open covenants of peace, openly arrived at, after which there shall be no private international understandings of any kind but diplomacy shall proceed always frankly and in the public view.

II.   Absolute freedom of navigation upon the seas, outside territorial waters, alike in peace and in war, except as the seas may be closed in whole or in part by international action for the enforcement of international covenants.

III.   The removal, so far as possible, of all economic barriers and the establishment of an equality of trade conditions among all the nations consenting to the peace and associating themselves for its maintenance.

IV.   Adequate guarantees given and taken that national armaments will be reduced to the lowest point consistent with domestic safety.

V.   A free, open-minded, and absolutely impartial adjustment of all colonial claims, based upon a strict observance of the principle that in determining all such questions of sovereignty the interests of the populations concerned must have equal weight with the equitable claims of the government whose title is to be determined.

VI.   The evacuation of all Russian territory and such a settlement of all questions affecting Russia as will secure the best and freest co-operation of the other nations of the world in obtaining for her an unhampered and unembarrassed opportunity for the independent determination of her own political development and national policy and assure her of a sincere welcome into the society of free nations under institutions of her own choosing; and, more than a welcome, assistance also of every kind that she may need and may herself desire. The treatment accorded Russia her sister nations in the months to come will be the acid test of their good will, of their comprehension of her needs as distinguished from their own interests, and of their intelligent and unselfish sympathy.

VII.   Belgium, the whole world will agree, must be evacuated and restored, without any attempt to limit the sovereignty which she enjoys in common with all other free nations. No other single act will serve as this will serve to restore confidence among the nations in the laws which they have themselves set and determined for the government of their relations with one another. Without this healing act the whole structure and validity of international law is forever impaired.

VIII.   All French territory should be freed and the invaded portions restored, and the wrong done to France by Prussia in 1871 in the matter of Alsace-Lorraine, which has unsettled the peace of the world for nearly fifty years, should be righted, in order that peace may ones more be made secure in the interest of all.

IX.   A readjustment of the frontiers of Italy should be effected along clearly recognizable lines of nationality.

X.   The peoples of Austria-Hungary, whose place among the nations we wish to see safeguarded and assured, should be accorded the freest opportunity of autonomous development.

XI.   Rumania, Serbia, and Montenegro should be evacuated: occupied territories restored: Serbia accorded free and secure access to the sea; and the relations of the several Balkan states to one another determined by friendly counsel along historically established lines of allegiance and nationality; and international guarantees of the political and economic independence and territorial integrity of the several Balkan states should be entered into.

XII.   The Turkish portions of the present Ottoman Empire should be assured a secure sovereignty, but the other nationalities which are now under Turkish rule should be assured an undoubted security of life and an absolutely unmolested opportunity of autonomous development, and the Dardanelles should be permanently opened as a free passage to the ships and commerce of all nations under international guarantees.

XIII.   An independent Polish state should be erected which should include the territories inhabited by indisputably Polish populations, which should be assured a free and secure access to the sea, and whose political and economic independence and territorial integrity should be guaranteed by international covenant.

XIV.   A general association of nations must be formed under specific covenant for the purpose of affording mutual guarantees of political independence and territorial integrity to great and small states alike.

In regard to these essential rectifications of wrong and assertions of right we feel ourselves to be intimate partners of all the governments and peoples associated together against the Imperialists. We cannot be separated in interest or divided in purpose. We stand together until the end.

For such arrangements and covenants we are willing to fight and to continue to fight until they are achieved; but only because we wish the right to prevail and desire a just and stable peace such as can be secured only by removing the chief provocations to war which this programme does remove. We have no jealousy of German greatness, and there is nothing in this programme that impairs it. We grudge her no achievement or distinction of learning or of pacific enterprise such as have made her record very bright and very enviable. We do not wish to injure her or to block in any way her legitimate influence or power. We do not wish to fight her either with arms or with hostile arrangements of trade if she is willing to associate herself with us and the other peace-loving nations of the world in covenants of justice and law and fair dealing. We wish her only to accept a place of equality among the peoples of the world, —the new world in which we now live—instead of a place of mastery.

Neither do we presume to suggest to her any alteration or modification of her institutions. But it is necessary, we must frankly say and necessary as a preliminary to any intelligent dealings with her on our part, that we should know whom her spokesmen speak for when they speak to us, whether for the Reichstag majority or for the military party and the men whose creed is imperial domination.

We have spoken now, surely, in terms too concrete to admit of any further doubt or question. An evident principle runs through the whole programme I have outlined. It is the principle of justice to all peoples and nationalities, and their right to live on equal terms of liberty and safety with one another, whether they be strong or weak. Unless this principle be made its foundation no part of the structure of international justice can stand. The people of the United States could act upon no other principle; and to the vindication of this principle they are ready to devote their lives, their honour, and everything that they possess. The moral climax of this the culminating and final war for human liberty has come, and they are ready to put their own strength, their own highest purpose, their own integrity and devotion to the test.

Address to Congress, January 8, 1918.

IV. Social Justice

Obligations of the State

We see that in many things life is very great. It is incomparably great in its material aspects, in its body of wealth, in the diversity and sweep of its energy, in the industries which have been conceived and built up by the genius of individual men and the limitless enterprise of groups of men. It is great, also, very great, in its moral force. Nowhere else in the world have noble men and women exhibited in more striking forms the beauty and the energy of sympathy and helpfulness and counsel in their efforts to rectify wrong, alleviate suffering, and set the weak in the way of strength and hope. We have built up, moreover, a great system of government, which has stood through a long age as in many respects a model for those who seek to set liberty upon foundations that will endure against fortuitous change, against storm and accident. Our life contains every great thing, and contains it in rich abundance.

But the evil has come with the good, and much fine gold has been corroded. With riches has come inexcusable waste. We have squandered a great part of what we might have used, and have not stopped to conserve the exceeding bounty of nature, without which our genius for enterprise would have been worthless and impotent, scorning to be careful, shamefully prodigal as well as admirably efficient. We have been proud of our industrial achievements, but we have not hitherto stopped thoughtfully enough to count the human cost, the cost of lives snuffed out, of energies overtaxed and broken, the fearful physical and spiritual cost to the men and women and children upon whom the dead weight and burden of it all has fallen pitilessly the years through. The groans and agony of it all had not yet reached our ears, the solemn, moving undertone of our life, coming up out of the mines and factories and out of every home where the struggle had its intimate and familiar seat. With the great Government went many deep secret things which we too long delayed to look into and scrutinize with candid, fearless eyes. The great Government we loved has too often been made use of for private and selfish purposes, and those who used it had forgotten the people.

At last a vision has been vouchsafed us of our life as a whole. We see the bad with the good, the debased and decadent with the sound and vital. With this vision we approach new affairs. Our duty is to cleanse, to reconsider, to restore, to correct the evil without impairing the good, to purify and humanize every process of our common life without weakening or sentimentalizing it.

There has been something crude and heartless and unfeeling in our haste to succeed and be great. Our thought has been "Let every man look out for himself, let every generation look out for itself," while we reared giant machinery which made it impossible that any but those who stood at the levers of control should have a chance to look out for themselves. We had not forgotten our morals. We remembered well enough that we had set up a policy which was meant to serve the humblest as well as the most powerful, with an eye single to the standards of justice and fair play, and remembered it with pride. But we were very heedless and in a hurry to be great.

We have come now to the sober second thought. The scales of heedlessness have fallen from our eyes. We have made up our minds to square every process of our national life again with the standards we so proudly set up at the beginning and have always carried at our hearts. Our work is a work of restoration.

We have itemized with some degree of particularity the things that ought to be altered and here are some of the chief items: A tariff which cuts us off from our proper part in the commerce of the world, violates the just principle of taxation, and makes the Government a facile instrument in the hands of private interests; a banking and currency system based upon the necessity of the Government to sell its bonds fifty years ago and perfectly adapted to concentrating cash and restricting credits; an industrial system which, take it on all its sides, financial as well as administrative, holds capital in leading strings, restricts the liberties and limits the opportunities of labour, and exploits without renewing or conserving the natural resources of the country; a body of agricultural activities never yet given the efficiency of great business undertakings or served as it should be through the instrumentality of science taken directly to the farm, or afforded the facilities of credit best suited to its practical needs; watercourses undeveloped, waste places unreclaimed, forests untended, fast disappearing without plan or prospect of renewal, unregarded waste heaps at every mine. We have studied as perhaps no other nation has the most effective means of production, but we have not studied cost or economy as we should either as organizers of industry, as statesmen, or as individuals.

Nor have we studied and perfected the means by which the government may be put at the service of humanity, in safeguarding the health of the nation, the health of its men and its women and its children, as well as their rights in the struggle for existence. This is no sentimental duty. The firm basis of government is justice, not pity. These are matters of justice. There can be no equality of opportunity, the first essential of justice in the body politic; if men and women and children be not shielded in their lives, their very vitality, from the consequences of great industrial and social processes which they cannot alter, control, or singly cope with. Society must see to it that it does not itself crush or weaken or damage its own constituent parts. The first duty of law is to keep sound the society it serves. Sanitary laws, pure food laws, and laws determining conditions of labour which individuals are powerless to determine for themselves are intimate parts of the very business of justice and legal efficiency.

These are some of the things we ought to do, and not leave the others undone, the old-fashioned, never-to-be-neglected, fundamental safeguarding of property and of individual right. This is the high enterprise of the new day: To lift everything that concerns our life as a Nation to the light that shines from the hearth fire of every man's conscience and vision of the right. It is inconceivable that we should do this as partisans; it is inconceivable we should do it in ignorance of the facts as they are or in blind haste. We shall restore, not destroy. We shall deal with our economic system as it is and as it may be modified, not as it might be if we had a clean sheet of paper to write upon; and step by step we shall make it what it should be, in the spirit of those who question their own wisdom and seek counsel and knowledge, not shallow, self-satisfaction or the excitement of excursions whither they cannot tell. Justice and only justice, shall always be our motto.

And yet it will be no cool process of mere science. The Nation has been deeply stirred, stirred by a solemn passion, stirred by the knowledge of wrong, of ideals lost, of government too often debauched and made an instrument of evil. The feelings with which we face this new age of right and opportunity sweep across our heartstrings like some air out of God's own presence, where justice and mercy are reconciled and the judge and the brother are one. We know our task to be no mere task of politics, but a task which shall search us through and through, whether we be able to understand our time and the need of our people, whether we be indeed their spokesmen and interpreters, whether we have the pure heart to comprehend and the rectified will to choose our high course of action.

First Inaugural Address. March 4, 1913.

The Spirit of Community

What has got to pervade us like a great motive power is that we cannot, and must not, separate our interests from one another, but must pool our interests. A man who is trying to fight for his single hand is fighting against the community and not fighting with it. There are a great many dreadful things about war, as nobody needs to be told in this day of distress and of terror, but there is one thing about war which has a very splendid side, and that is the consciousness that a whole nation gets that they must all act as a unit for a common end. And when peace is as handsome as war there will be no war. When men, I mean, engage in the pursuits of peace in the same spirit of self-sacrifice and of conscious service of the community with which, at any rate, the common soldier engages in war, then shall there be wars no more.

Address to the U. S. Chamber of Commerce, at Washington, February 3, 1915.

The Path of Conciliation

While we are fighting for freedom we must see, among other things, that labour is free; and that means a number of interesting things. It means not only that we must do what we have declared our purpose to do, see that the conditions of labour are not rendered more onerous by the war, but also that we shall see to it that the instrumentalities by which the conditions of labour are improved are not blocked or checked. That we must do...

Now, to stand together means that nobody must interrupt the processes of our energy if the interruption can possibly be avoided without the absolute invasion of freedom. To put it concretely, that means this: Nobody has a right to stop the processes of labour until all the methods of conciliation and settlement have been exhausted. And I might as well say right here that I am not talking to you alone. You sometimes stop the courses of labour, but there are others who do the same, and I believe I am speaking from my own experience not only, but from the experience of others when I say that you are reasonable in a larger number of cases than the capitalists. I am not saying these things to them personally yet, because I have not had a chance, but they have to be said, not in any spirit of criticism, but in order to clear the atmosphere and come down to business. Everybody on both sides has now got to transact business, and a settlement is never impossible when both sides want to do the square and right thing.

Moreover, a settlement is always hard to avoid when the parties can be brought face to face. I can differ from a man much more radically when he is not in the room than I can when he is in the room, because then the awkward thing is he can come back at me and answer what I say. It is always dangerous for a man to have the floor entirely to himself. Therefore, we must insist in every instance that the parties come into each other's presence

and there discuss the issues between them, and not separately in places which have no communication with
each other... We are all of the same clay and spirit, and
we can get together if we desire to get together.

*Address to the American Federation of Labour Conven-
tion, at Buffalo. November 12. 1917.*

All Men must be Free

You have, then, this noble picture of justice and mercy as
the two servants of liberty. For only where men are free
do they think the thoughts of comradeship, only where
they are free do they think the thoughts of sympathy,
only where they are free are they mutually helpful only
where they are free do they realize their dependence
upon one another and their comradeship in a common
interest and common necessity. If you ladies and gentlemen could read some of the touching despatches which
come through official channels, for even through those
channels there come voices of humanity that are infin-
itely pathetic; if you could catch some of those voices
that speak the utter longing of oppressed and helpless
peoples all over the world to hear something like the
Battle Hymn of the Republic, to hear the feet of the great
hosts of Liberty coming to set them free, to set their
minds free, set their lives free, set their children free; you
would know what comes into the heart of those who are
trying to contribute all the brains and power they have to
this great enterprise of Liberty.

Address to the Public Meeting in New York. Opening a Campaign for the Second Red Cross Fund, May 18, 1918.

V. Towards International Order

Force of Public Opinion

The opinion of the world is the mistress of the world; and the processes of international law are the slow processes by which opinion works its will. What impresses me is the constant thought that that is the tribunal at the bar of which we all sit. I would call your attention, incidentally, to the circumstance that it does not observe the ordinary rules of evidence; which has sometimes suggested to me that the ordinary rules of evidence had shown some signs of growing antique. Everything, rumour included, is heard in this court, and the standard of judgment is not so much the character of the testimony as the character of the witnesses. The motives are disclosed, the purposes are conjectured, and that opinion is finally accepted which seems to be, not the best founded in law, perhaps, but the best founded in integrity of character and morals. That is the process which is slowly working its will upon the world; and what we should be watchful of is not so much jealous interests as sound principles of action. The disinterested course is always the biggest course to pursue not only, but it is in the long run the most profitable course to pursue. If you can establish your character you can establish your credit.

Address before the American Bar Association, October 20, 1914.

The Basis of Common Interest

The longer the war lasts, the more deeply do we become concerned that it should be brought to an end and the world be permitted to resume its normal life and course again. And when it does come to an end we shall be as much concerned as the nations at war to see peace assume an aspect of permanence, give promise of days from which the anxiety of uncertainty shall be lifted, bring some assurance that peace and war shall always hereafter be reckoned part of the common interest of mankind. We are participants, whether we would or not, in the life of the world. The interests of all nations are our own also. We are partners with the rest. What affects mankind is inevitably our affair as well as the affair of the nations of Europe and of Asia.

... Only when the great nations of the world have reached some sort of agreement as to what they hold to be fundamental to their common interest, and as to some feasible method of acting in concert when any nation or group of nations seeks to disturb those fundamental things, can we feel that civilization is at last in a way of justifying its existence and claiming to be finally established. It is clear that nations must in the future be governed by the same high code of honour that we demand of individuals.

We must, indeed, in the very same breath with which we avow this conviction admit that we have ourselves upon occasion in the past been offenders against the law of diplomacy which we thus forecast; but our conviction is not the less clear, but rather the more clear, on that account. If the war has accomplished nothing else for the benefit of the world, it has at least disclosed a great moral necessity and set forward the thinking of the statesmen of the world by a whole age. Repeated utterances of the leading statesmen of most of the great nations now engaged in war have made it plain that their thought has come to this, that the principle of public right must henceforth take precedence over the individual interests of particular nations, and that the nations of the world must in some way band themselves together to sec that the right prevails as against any sort of selfish aggression; that henceforth alliance must not be set up against alliance, understanding against understanding, but that there must be a common agreement for a common object, and that at the heart of that common object must lie the inviolable rights of peoples and of mankind. The nations of the world have become each other's neighbours. It is to their interest that they should understand each other. In order that they may understand each other, it is imperative that they should agree to co-operate in a common cause, and that they should so act that the guiding principle of that common cause shall be even-handed and impartial justice.

This is undoubtedly the thought of America. This is what we ourselves will say when there comes proper occasion to say it. In the dealings of nations with one another arbitrary force must be rejected and we must move forward to the thought of the modern world, the thought of which peace is the very atmosphere. That thought constitutes a chief part of the passionate conviction of America.

We believe these fundamental things: First, that every people has a right to choose the sovereignty under which they shall live. Like other nations, we have ourselves no doubt once and again offended against that principle when for a little while controlled by selfish passion, as our franker historians have been honourable enough to admit: but it has become more and more our rule of life and action. Second, that the small states of the world have a right to enjoy the same respect for their sovereignty and for their territorial integrity that great and powerful nations expect and insist upon. And, third, that the world has a right to be free from every disturbance of its peace that has its origin in aggression and disregard of the rights of peoples and nations.

So sincerely do we believe in these things that I am sure that I speak the mind and wish of the people of America when I say that the United States is willing to become a partner in any feasible association of. nations formed in order to realize these objects and, make them secure against violation.

There is nothing that the United States wants for itself that; any other nation has. We are willing, on the contrary, to limit ourselves along with them to a prescribed course of duty and respect for the rights of others which will check any selfish passion of our own, as it will check any aggressive impulse of theirs.

If it should ever be our privilege to suggest or initiate a movement for peace among the nations now at war, I am sure that the people of the United States would wish their Government to move along these lines: First, such a settlement with regard to their own immediate interests as the belligerents may agree upon. We have nothing material of any kind to ask for ourselves, and are quite aware that we are in no sense or degree parties to the present quarrel. Our interest is only in peace and its future guarantees. Second, an universal association of the nations to maintain the inviolable security of the highway of the seas for the common and unhindered use of all the nations of the world, and to prevent any war begun either contrary to treaty covenants or without warning and full submission of the causes to the opinion of the world—a virtual guarantee of territorial integrity and political independence.

But I did not come here, let me repeat, to discuss a programme. I came only to avow a creed and give expression to the confidence I feel that the world is even now upon the eve of a great consummation, when some common force will be brought into existence which shall safeguard right as the first and most fundamental interest of all peoples and all governments, when coercion shall be summoned not to the service of political ambition or selfish hostility; but to the service of a common order, a common justice, and a common peace. God grant that the dawn of that day of frank dealing and of settled peace, concord, and co-operation may be near at hand!

Address to the League to Enforce Peace at Washington, May 27, 1916.

A Society of Nations

...What I intend to preach from this time on is that America must show that as a member of the family of nations she has the same attitude toward the other nations that she wishes her people to have toward each other: That America is going to take this position, that she will lend her moral influence, not only, but her physical force, if other nations will join her to see to it that no nation or group of nations, tries to take advantage of another nation or group of nations, and that the only thing ever fought for is the common rights of humanity...

Have you ever heard what started the present war? If you have, I wish you would publish it, because nobody else has, so far as I can gather. Nothing in particular started it, but everything in general. There had been growing up in Europe a mutual suspicion, an interchange of conjectures about what this Government and that Government was going to do, an interlacing of alliances and understandings, a complex web of intrigue and spying, that presently was sure to entangle the whole of the family of mankind on that side of the water in its meshes.

Now, revive that after this war is over and sooner or later you will have just such another war, and this is the last war of the kind or of any kind that involves the world that the United States can keep out of.

I say that because I believe that the business of neutrality is over; not because I want it to be over, but I mean this, that war now has such a scale that the position of neutrals sooner or later becomes intolerable. Just as neutrality would be intolerable to me if I lived in a community where everybody had to assert his own right by force and I had to go around among my neighbours and say: "Here, this cannot last any longer; let us get together and see that nobody disturbs the peace any more." That is what society is and we have not yet a society of nations.

We must have a society of nations, not suddenly, not by insistence, not by any hostile emphasis upon the demand, but by the demonstration of the needs of the time. The nations of the world must get together and say, "Nobody can hereafter be neutral as respects the disturbance of the world's peace for an object which the world's opinion cannot sanction." The world's peace ought to be disturbed if the fundamental rights of humanity are invaded, but it ought not to be disturbed for any other thing that I can think of, and America was established in order to indicate, at any rate in one Government, the fundamental rights of man. America must hereafter be ready as a member of the family of nations to exert her whole force, moral and physical, to the assertion of those lights throughout the round globe.

Address at Cincinnati, October 26, 1916.

Principles of a Liberated Mankind

... We realize that the greatest things that remain to be done must be done with the whole world for stage and co-operation with the wide and universal forces of mankind, and we are making our spirits ready for those things. They will follow in the immediate wake of the war itself and will set civilization up again. We are provincials no longer. The tragical events of the thirty months of vital turmoil through which we have just passed have made us citizens of the world. There can be no turning back. Our own fortunes as a nation are involved, whether we would have it so or not.

And yet we are not the less American on that account. We shall be the more American if we but remain true to the principles in which we have been bred. They are not the principles of a province or of a single continent. We have known and boasted all along that they were the principles of a liberated mankind. These, therefore, are the things we shall stand for, whether in war or in peace:

That all nations are equally interested in the peace of the world and in the political stability of free peoples, and equally responsible for their maintenance;

That the essential principle of peace is the actual equality of nations in all matters of right or privilege;

That peace cannot securely or justly rest upon an armed balance of power;

That governments derive all their just powers from the consent of the governed and that no other powers should be supported by the common thought, purpose, or power of the family of nations;

That the seas should be equally free and safe for the use of all peoples, under rules set up by common agreement and consent, and that, so far as practicable, they should be accessible to all upon equal terms;

That national armaments should be limited to the necessities of. national order and domestic safety;

That the community of interest and of power upon which peace must henceforth depend imposes upon each nation the duty of seeing to it that all influences proceeding from its own citizens meant to encourage or assist revolution in other states should be sternly and effectually suppressed and prevented.

Second Inaugural Address, March 5, 1917.

Fundamentals of a Reign of Law

... There must now be settled, once for all, what was settled for America in the great age upon whose inspiration we draw to-day. This is surely a fitting place from which calmly to look upon our task, that we may fortify our spirits for its accomplishment. And this is the appropriate place from which to avow, alike to the friends who look on and to the friends with whom we have the happiness to be associated in action, the faith and purpose with which we act.

This, then, is our conception of the great struggle in which we are engaged. The plot is written plain upon every scene and every act of the supreme tragedy. On the one hand stand the peoples of the world—not only the peoples actually engaged, but many others also, who suffer under mastery but cannot act; peoples of many races and in every part of the world—the people of stricken Russia still, among the rest, though they are for the moment unorganised and helpless. Opposed to them, masters of many armies, stand an isolated, friendless group of Governments, who speak no common purpose, but only selfish ambitions of their own, by which none can profit but themselves, and whose peoples are fuel in their hands; Governments which fear their people, and yet are for the time being sovereign lords, making every choice for them and disposing of their lives and fortunes as they will, as well as of the lives and fortunes of every people who fall under their power—Governments clothed with the strange trappings and the primitive authority of an age that is altogether alien and hostile to our own. The Past and the Present are in deadly grapple, and the peoples of the world are being done to death between them.

There can be but one issue. The settlement must be final. There can be no compromise. No halfway decision would be tolerable. No halfway decision is conceivable. These are the ends for which the associated peoples of the world are fighting and which must be conceded them before there can be peace:

I. —The destruction of every arbitrary power anywhere that can separately, secretly, and of its single choice disturb the peace of the world; or, if it cannot be presently destroyed, at least its reduction to virtual impotence;

II. —The settlement of every question, whether of territory, of sovereignty, of economic arrangement, or of political relationship, upon the basis of the free acceptance of that settlement by the people immediately concerned, and not upon the basis of the material interest or advantage of any other nation or people which may desire a different settlement for the sake of its own exterior influence or mastery.

III. —The consent of all nations to be governed in their conduct toward each other by the same principles of honour and of respect for the common law of civilized society that govern the individual citizens of all modern States in their relations with one another; to the end that all promises and covenants may be sacredly observed, no private plots or conspiracies hatched, no selfish injuries wrought with impunity, and a mutual trust established upon the handsome foundation of a mutual respect of right.

IV. —The establishment of an organization of peace which shall make it certain that the combined power of free nations will check every invasion of right and serve to make peace and justice the more secure by affording a definite tribunal of opinion to which all must submit and by which every international readjustment that Cannot be amicably agreed upon by the peoples directly concerned shall be sanctioned.

These great objects can be put into a single sentence. What we seek is the reign of law, based upon the consent of the governed and sustained by the organized opinion of mankind.

These great ends cannot be achieved by debating and seeking to reconcile and accommodate what statesmen may wish with their projects for balances of power and of national opportunity. They can be realized only by the determination of what the thinking peoples of the world desire, with their longing hope for justice and for social freedom and opportunity.

Address at Mount Vernon, July 4, 1918.

League of Nations and a Peoples' Peace

At every turn of the war we gain a fresh consciousness of what we mean to accomplish by it. When our hope and expectation are most excited we think more definitely than before of the issues that hang upon it and of the purposes which must be realized by means of it. For it has positive and well-defined purposes which we did not determine and which we cannot alter. No statesman or assembly created them; no statesman or assembly can alter them. They have arisen out of the very nature and circumstances of the war. The most that statesmen or assemblies can do is to carry them out or be false to them. They were perhaps not clear at the outset; but they are clear now. The war has lasted more than four years and the whole world has been drawn into it. The common will of mankind has been substituted for the particular purposes of individual States. Individual statesmen may have started the conflict, but neither they nor their opponents can stop it as they please. It has become a peoples' war, and peoples of all sorts and races, of every degree of power and variety of fortune, are involved in its sweeping processes of change and settlement. We came into it when its character had become fully defined and it was plain that no nation could stand apart or be indifferent to its outcome. Its challenge drove to the heart of everything we cared for and lived for. The voice of the war had become clear and gripped our hearts. Our brothers from many lands, as well as our own murdered dead under the sea, were calling to us, and we responded, fiercely and of course.

The air was clear about us. We saw things in their full, convincing proportions as they were; and we have seen them with steady eyes and unchanging comprehension ever since. We accepted the issues of the war as facts, not as any group of men either here or elsewhere had defined them, and we can accept no outcome which does not squarely meet and settle them. Those issues are these:

Shall the military power of any nation or group of nations be suffered to determine the fortunes of peoples over whom they have no right to rule except the right of force?

Shall strong nations be free to wrong weak nations and make them subject to their purpose and interest?

Shall peoples be ruled and dominated, even in their own internal affairs, by arbitrary and irresponsible force or by their own will and choice?

Shall there be a common standard of right and privilege for all peoples and nations or shall the strong do as they will and the weak suffer without redress?

Shall the assertion of right be haphazard and by casual alliance or shall there be a common concert to oblige the observance of common rights?

No man, no group of men chose these to be the issues of the struggle. They are the issues of it; and they must be settled—by no arrangement or compromise or adjustment of interests, but definitely and once for all and with a full and unequivocal acceptance of the principle that the interest of the weakest is as sacred as the interest of the strongest.

This is what we mean when we speak of a permanent peace, if we speak sincerely, intelligently, and with a real knowledge and comprehension of the matter we deal with...

It is of capital importance that we should also be explicitly agreed that no peace shall be obtained by any kind of compromise or abatement of the principles we have avowed as the principles for which we are fighting. There should exist no doubt about that. I am, therefore, going to take the liberty of speaking with the utmost frankness about the practical implications that are involved in it.

If it be indeed and in truth the common object of the Governments associated against Germany and of the nations whom they govern, as I believe it to be, to achieve by the coming settlements a secure and lasting peace, it will be necessary that all who sit down at the peace table shall come ready and willing to pay the price, the only price, that will procure it; and ready and willing, also, to create in some virile fashion the only instrumentality by which it can be made certain that the agreements of the peace will be honoured and fulfilled.

That price is impartial justice in every item of the settlement, no matter whose interest is crossed; and not only impartial justice but also the satisfaction of the several peoples whose fortunes are dealt with. That indispensable instrumentality is a League of Nations formed under covenants that will be efficacious. Without such an instrumentality, by which the peace of the world can be guaranteed, peace will rest in part upon the word of outlaws, and only upon that word. For Germany will have to redeem her character, not by what happens at the peace table but by what follows...

But these general terms do not disclose the whole matter. Some details are needed to make them sound less like a thesis and more like a practical programme. These, then, arc some of the particulars, and I state them with the greater confidence because I can state them authoritatively as representing this Government's interpretation of its own duty with regard to peace;

First, the impartial justice meted out must involve no discrimination between those to whom we wish to be just and those to whom we do not wish to be just. It must be a justice that plays no favourites and knows no standard but the equal rights of the several peoples concerned;

Second, no special or separate interest of any single nation or any group of nations can be made the basis of any part of the settlement which is not consistent with the common interest of all;

Third, there can be no leagues or alliances or special covenants and understandings within the general and common family of the League of Nations;

Fourth, and more specifically, there can be no special, selfish economic combinations within the league and no employment of any form of economic boycott or exclusion except as the power of economic penalty by exclusion from the markets of the world may be vested in the

League of Nations itself as a means of discipline and control;

Fifth, all international agreements and treaties of every kind must be made known in their entirety to the rest of the world.

Special alliances and economic rivalries and hostilities have been the prolific source in the modern world of the plans and passions that produce war. It would be an insincere as well as an insecure peace that did not exclude them in definite and binding terms.

The confidence with which I venture to speak for our people in these matters docs not spring from our traditions merely and the well-known principles of international action which we have always professed and followed. In the same sentence in which I say that the United States will enter into no special arrangements or understandings with particular nations let me say also that the United States is prepared to assume its full share of responsibility for the maintenance of the common covenants and understandings upon which peace must henceforth rest. We still read Washington's immortal warning against "entangling alliances" with full comprehension and an answering purpose. But only special and limited alliances entangle; and we recognize and accept the duty of a new day in which we are permitted to hope for a general alliance which will avoid entanglements and clear the air of the world for common understandings and the maintenance of common rights.

I have made this analysis of the international situation which the war has created, not, of course, because I doubted whether the leaders of the great nations and peoples with whom we are associated were of the same mind and entertained a like purpose, but because the air every now and again gets darkened by mists and groundless doubtings and mischievous perversions of counsel and it is necessary once and again to sweep all the irresponsible talk about peace intrigues and weakening morale and doubtful purpose on the part of those in authority utterly, and if need be unceremoniously, aside and say things in the plainest words that can be found, even when it is only to say over again what has been said before, quite as plainly if in less unvarnished terms.

As I have said, neither I nor any other man in governmental authority created or gave form to the issues of this war. I have simply responded to them with such vision as I could command. But I have responded gladly and with a resolution that has grown warmer and more confident as the issues have grown clearer and clearer It is now plain that they are issues which no man can pervert unless it be wilfully. I am bound to fight for them, and happy to fight for them as time and circumstance have revealed them to me as to all the world. Our enthusiasm for them grows more and more irresistible as they stand out in more and more vivid and unmistakable outline.

And the forces that fight for them draw into closer and closer array, organize their millions into more and more unconquerable might, as they become more and more distinct to the thought and purpose of the peoples engaged. It is the peculiarity of this great war that while statesmen have seemed to cast about for definitions of their purpose and have sometimes seemed to shift their ground and their point of view, the thought of the mass of men, whom statesmen are supposed to instruct and lead, has grown more and more unclouded, more and more certain of what it is they are fighting for. National purposes have fallen more and more into the background and the common purpose of enlightened mankind has taken their place. The counsels of plain men have become on all hands more simple and straightforward and more unified than the counsels of sophisticated men of affairs, who still retain the impression that they are playing a game of power and playing for high stakes. That is why I have said that this is a peoples' war, not a statesman's. Statesmen must follow the clarified common thought or be broken.

I take that to be the significance of the fact that assemblies and associations of many kinds made up of plain workaday people have demanded, almost every time they came together, and are still demanding, that the leaders of their Governments declare to them plainly what it is, exactly what it is, that they are seeking in this war, and what they think the items of the final settlement should be. They are not yet satisfied with what they have been told. They still seem to fear that they are getting what they ask for only in statesmen's terms—only in the terms of territorial arrangements and divisions of power, and not in terms of broad-visioned justice and mercy and peace and the satisfaction of those deep-seated longings of oppressed and distracted men and women and enslaved peoples that seem to them the only things worth fighting a war for that engulfs the world. Perhaps statesmen have not always recognized this changed aspect of the whole world of policy and action. Perhaps they have not always spoken in direct reply to questions asked because they did not know how searching those questions were and what sort of answers they demanded.

But I, for one, am glad to attempt the answer again and again, in the hope that I may make it clearer and clearer that my one thought is to satisfy those who struggle in the ranks and are, perhaps above all others, entitled to a reply whose meaning no one can have any excuse for misunderstanding, if he understands the language in which it is spoken or can get someone to translate it correctly into his own. And I believe that the leaders of the Governments with which we are associated will speak as they have occasion as plainly as I have tried to speak. I hope that they will feel free to say whether they think that I am in any degree mistaken in my interpretation of the issues involved or in my purpose with regard to the means by which a satisfactory settlement of those issues may be obtained. Unity of purpose and of counsel are as imperatively necessary in this war as was unity of command in the battlefield; and with perfect unity of purpose and counsel will come assurance of complete victory. It can be had in no other way. "Peace drives" can be effectively neutralized and silenced only by showing that every victory of the nations associated against Germany brings the nations nearer the sort of peace which will bring security and reassurance to all peoples and make the recurrence of another such struggle of pitiless force and bloodshed forever impossible, and that nothing else can. Germany is constantly intimating the "terms" she will accept; and always finds that the world does not want terms. It wishes the final triumph of justice and fair dealing.

Address to Public Meeting in New York, Opening the Fourth Liberty Loan, September 27, 1918.

VI. Post-War Reconstruction

So far as our domestic affairs are concerned, the problem of our return to peace is a problem of economic and industrial readjustment. That problem is less serious for us than it may turn out to be for the nations which have suffered the disarrangements and the losses of the war longer than we. Our people, moreover, do not wait to be coached and led. They know their own business, are quick and resourceful at every readjustment, definite in purpose, and self-reliant in action. Any leading strings we might seek to put them in would speedily become hopelessly tangled, because they would pay no attention to them, and go their own way. All that we can do as their legislative and executive servants is to mediate the process of change here, there, and elsewhere, as we may. I have heard much counsel as to the plans that should be formed and personally conducted to a happy consummation, but from no quarter have I seen any general scheme of "reconstruction" emerge which I thought it likely we could force our spirited business men and self-reliant labourers to accept with due pliancy and obedience.

While the war lasted we set up many agencies by which to direct the industries of the country in the services it was necessary for them to render, by which to make sure of an abundant supply of materials needed by which to check undertakings that could for the time be dispensed with, and stimulate those that were most serviceable in war, by which to gain for the purchasing departments of the government a certain control over the prices of essential articles and materials, by which to restrain trade with alien enemies, make the most of the available shipping, and systematize financial transactions, both public and private, so that there would be no unnecessary conflict or confusion—by which, in short, to put every material energy of the country in harness to draw the common load and make of us one team in the accomplishment of a great task. But the moment we knew the armistice to have been signed we took the harness off. Raw materials, upon which the Government had kept its hand for fear there should not be enough for the industries that supplied the armies, have been released and put into the general market again. Great industrial plants whose whole output and machinery had been taken over for the uses of the Government have been set free to return to the uses to which they were put before the war. It has not been possible to remove so readily or so quickly the control of foodstuffs and of shipping, because the world has still to be fed from our granaries and the ships are still needed to send supplies to our men overseas, and to bring the men back as far as the disturbed conditions on the other side of the water permit. But even these restraints are being relaxed as much as possible, and more and more as the weeks go by.

Never before have there been agencies in existence in this country which knew so much of the field of supply, of labour, and of industry as the War Industries Board, the War Trade Board, the Labour Department, the Food Administration and the Fuel Administration have known since the labours became thoroughly systematized, and they have not been isolated agencies. They have been directed by men that represented the permanent departments of the Government, and so have been the centres of unified and co-operative action. It has been the policy of the Executive, therefore, since the armistice (which is in effect a complete submission of the enemy), to put the knowledge of these bodies at the disposal of the business men of the country, and to offer their intelligent mediation at every point and in every matter where it was desired. It is surprising how fast the process of return to a peace footing has moved in the three weeks since the fighting stopped. It promises to outrun any inquiry that may be instituted and any aid that may be offered. It will not be easy to direct it any better than it will direct itself. The American business man is of quick initiative.

The ordinary and normal processes of private initiatives will not, however, provide immediate employment for all of the men of our returning armies. Those who are of trained capacity, those who are skilled workmen, those who have acquired familiarity with established businesses, those who are ready and willing to go to the farms, all those whose aptitudes are known or will be sought out by employers, will find no difficulty, it is safe to say, in finding place and employment. But there will be others who will be at a loss where to gain a livelihood unless pains are taken to guide them and put them in the way of work. There will be a large floating residuum of labour which should not be left wholly to shift for itself. It seems to me important, therefore, that the development of public works of every sort should be promptly resumed, in order that opportunities should be created for unskilled labour in particular, and that plans should be made for such developments of our unused lands and our natural resources as we have hitherto lacked stimulation to undertake.

I particularly direct your attention to the very practical plans which the Secretary of the Interior has developed in his annual report, and before your committees for the reclamation of arid, swamp and cut-over lands, which might, if the States were willing and able to co-operate, redeem some three hundred million acres of land for cultivation. There are said to be fifteen or twenty million acres of land in the West, at present arid, for whose reclamation water is available, if properly conserved. There are about two hundred and thirty million acres from which the forests have been cut, but which have never yet been cleared for the plough, and which lie waste and desolate. These lie scattered all over the Union. And there are nearly eighty million acres of land that lie under swamps or subject to periodical overflow, or too wet for anything but grazing, which it is perfectly feasible to drain and protect and redeem. The Congress can at once direct thousands of the returning soldiers to the reclamation of the arid lands which it has already undertaken, if it will but enlarge the plans and the appropriations which it has entrusted to the Department of the Interior. It is possible in dealing with our unused land to effect a great rural and agricultural development, which will afford the best sort of opportunity to men who want to help themselves, and the Secretary of the Interior has thought the possible methods out in a way which is worthy of your most friendly attention.

I have spoken of the control which must yet for a while, perhaps for a long time, be exercised over shipping because of priority of service to which our forces overseas are entitled and which should also be accorded the shipments which are to save recently liberated peoples from starvation and many devastated regions from permanent ruin. May I not say a special word about the needs of Belgium and Northern France? No sums of money paid by way of indemnity will serve of themselves to save them from hopeless disadvantage for years to come. Something more must be done than merely find the money.

If they had money and raw materials in abundance tomorrow, they could not resume their place in the industry of the world tomorrow—the very important place they held before the flame of war swept across them. Many of their factories are razed to the ground. Much of their machinery is destroyed or has been taken away. Their people are scattered, and many of their best workmen are dead. Their markets will be taken by others, if they are not in some special way assisted to rebuild their factories and replace their lost instruments of manufacture. They should not be left to the vicissitudes of the sharp competition for materials and for industrial facilities which is now to set in.

I hope, therefore, that the Congress will not be unwilling, if it should become necessary, to grant to some such agency as the War Trade Board the right to establish priorities of export and supply for the benefit of these people whom we have been so happy to assist in saving from the German terror and whom we must not now thoughtlessly leave to shift for themselves in a pitiless competitive market.

Address to Congress. December 2, 1918.

The Threshold of World Order

And now we are sure of the great triumph for which every sacrifice was made. It has come—come in its completeness, and with the pride and inspiration of these days of achievement quick within us, we turn to the tasks of peace again—a peace secure against the violence of irresponsible monarchs and ambitious military coteries, and made ready for a new order, for new foundations of justice and fair dealing.

We are about to give order and organization to this peace, not only for ourselves but for the other peoples of the world as well, so far as they will suffer us to serve them...

I welcome this occasion to announce to the Congress my purpose to join in Paris the representatives of the Governments with which we have been associated in the war against the Central Empires for the purpose of discussing with them the main features of the treaty of peace. I realize the great inconveniences that will attend my leaving the country, particularly at this time, but the conclusion that it was my paramount duty to go has been forced upon me by considerations which I hope will seem as conclusive to you as they have seemed to me.

The Allied Governments have accepted the bases of peace which I outlined to the Congress on the 8th of January last, as the Central Empires also have, and very reasonably desire my personal counsel in their interpretation and application, and it is highly desirable that I should give it in order that the sincere desire of our Government to contribute without selfish purpose of any kind to settlements that will be made of common benefit to all the nations concerned may be made fully manifest. The peace settlements which are now to be agreed upon are of transcendent importance, both to us and to the rest of the world, and I know of no business or interest which should take precedence of them. The gallant men of our armed forces on land and sea have conspicuously fought for the ideals of their country. I have sought to express those ideals; they have accepted my statements of them as the substance of their own thought and purpose, as the associated Governments have accepted them; I owe it to them to see to it, so far as in me lies, that no false or mistaken interpretation is put upon them, and no possible effort omitted to realize them. It is now my duty to play my full part in making good what they offered their life's blood to obtain. I can think of no call to service which should transcend this.

Address to Congress, December 2, 1918.